Vocabulary
4000

JEFF KOLBY

NOVA
PRESS

Additional educational titles from Nova Press (available at novapress.net):

- ➢ **GRE Prep Course** (624 pages, includes software)
  GRE Math Prep Course (528 pages)
- ➢ **GMAT Prep Course** (624 pages, includes software)
  GMAT Math Prep Course (528 pages)
- ➢ **Master The LSAT** (608 pages, includes 4 official LSAT exams)
- ➢ **The MCAT Physics Book** (444 pages)
  The MCAT Biology Book (416 pages)
  The MCAT Chemistry Book (428 pages)
- ➢ **SAT Prep Course** (628 pages)
  SAT Math Prep Course (404 pages)
- ➢ **ACT Math Prep Course** (402 pages)
- ➢ **Speaking and Writing Strategies for the TOEFL® iBT:** (394 pages)
  500 Words, Phrases, and Idioms for the TOEFL® iBT: (238 pages)
- ➢ **Law School Basics:** A Preview of Law School and Legal Reasoning (224 pages)

Copyright © 2016 by Nova Press
Previous editions 2014, 2012, 2009, 2000, 1997
All rights reserved.

ISBN-10: 1–944595–22–8
ISBN-13: 978–1–944595–22–7

 **NOVA PRESS**

P. O. Box: 692023
West Hollywood, CA 90069

Phone: 1-310-275-3513
E-mail: info@novapress.net
Website: www.novapress.net

Contents

ABOUT THIS BOOK 5

THE WORDS 7

WORD ANALYSIS 103

IDIOM AND USAGE 117

About This Book

English offers perhaps the richest vocabulary of all languages, in part because its words are culled from so many languages. It is a shame that we do not tap this rich source more often in our daily conversation to express ourselves more clearly and precisely.

There are of course thesauruses but they mainly list common words. Other vocabulary books list difficult, esoteric words that we quickly forget or feel self-conscious using. However, there is a bounty of choice words between the common and the esoteric that often seem be just on the tip of our tongue. Vocabulary 4000 brings these words to the fore.

Whenever possible, one-word definitions are used. Although this makes a definition less precise, it also makes it easier to remember. Many common words appear in the list of words, but with their less common meanings. For example, the common meaning of *champion* is "winner." A less common meaning for *champion* is to support or fight for someone else. (Think of the phrase "to champion a cause.") This is the meaning that would be used in the list.

As you read through the list of words, mark any that you do not know with a check mark. Then when you read through the list again, mark any that you do not remember with two checks. Continue in this manner until you have learned the words.

There are four types of quizzes interspersed in the word list: Matching, Antonyms, Analogies, and Sentence Completions. The Matching quizzes, review words that were just introduced. All the other quizzes contain words from any part of the list.

THE
WORDS

A

a cappella without accompaniment

à la carte priced separately

a priori reasoning based on general principles

aback unexpected, surprised

abacus counting device

abandon desert, forsake

abase degrade

abash humiliate, embarrass

abate lessen, subside

abatement alleviation

abbey monastery

abbreviate shorten

abdicate relinquish power or position

abdomen belly

abduct kidnap

aberrant abnormal

abet aid, encourage (typically of crime)

abeyance postponement

abhor detest

abide submit, endure

abject wretched

abjure renounce

ablate cut away

ablution cleansing

abode home

abolish annul, eliminate

abominable detestable

aboriginal indigenous, native

abortive unsuccessful

abound be plentiful

abreast side-by-side

abridge shorten

abroad overseas

abrogate cancel

abrupt ending suddenly

abscess infected and inflamed tissue

abscond to run away (secretly)

absolve acquit, free from blame

abstain refrain

abstract theoretical, intangible

abstruse difficult to understand

abut touch, border on

abysmal deficient, sub par

abyss chasm

academy school

accede yield, agree

accentuate emphasize

accession attainment of rank

accessory attachment, accomplice

acclaim recognition, fame

acclimate accustom oneself to a climate, adjust

acclivity ascent, incline

accolade applause, tribute

accommodate adapt, assist, house

accomplice one who aids a lawbreaker

accord agreement

accost to approach and speak to someone aggressively

accouter equip, clothe

accredit authorize

accrete grow larger

accrue accumulate

accumulate amass

acerbic caustic, bitter (of speech)

acme summit, zenith

acolyte assistant (usually to clergy)

acoustic pertaining to sound

acquaint familiarize

acquiesce agree passively

acquit free from blame

acrid pungent, caustic, choking

acrimonious caustic, bitter, resentful

acrophobia fear of heights

actuate induce, start

acumen insight

acute sharp, intense

ad nauseam to a ridiculous degree

ad-lib improvise

adage proverb

adamant insistent

adapt adjust to changing conditions

adaptable pliable

addendum appendix, supplement

adduce offer as example

adept skillful

adhere stick to

adherent supporter

adieu farewell

adipose fatty

adjacent next to

adjourn suspend, discontinue

adjudicate judge

adjunct addition

administer manage

admissible allowable

admonish warn gently

ado fuss, commotion

Adonis a beautiful man

adroit skillful

adulation applause, worship

adulterate contaminate, corrupt

adumbration overshadow

advent arrival of something important

adventitious accidental, extrinsic

adversary opponent

adverse unfavorable, opposing

adversity hardship

advise give counsel

advocate urge, support

aegis that which protects, sponsorship

aerial pertaining to the air

aerobics exercise

Quiz 1 (Matching)

Match each word in the first column with its definition in the second column. Answers are on page 100.

1.	ABASE	A.	applause
2.	ABSTAIN	B.	caustic
3.	ACOLYTE	C.	shorten
4.	ABEYANCE	D.	applause
5.	ABRIDGE	E.	assistant
6.	ACCOLADE	F.	postponement
7.	ACRIMONIOUS	G.	refrain
8.	ADDUCE	H.	exercise
9.	ADULATION	I.	degrade
10.	AEROBICS	J.	offer as example

---

aesthetic pleasing to the senses, beautiful

affable friendly

affect influence

affectation pretense, showing off

affidavit sworn written statement

affiliate associate

affiliation connection, association

affinity fondness

affix fasten

affliction illness

affluent abundant, wealthy

affray brawl

affront insult

aficionado devotee, ardent follower

afoul entangled, in trouble

aft rear

aftermath consequence

agape wonder

agenda plan, timetable

agent provocateur agitator

aggrandize exaggerate

aggravate worsen

aggregate total, collect

aggressor attacker

aggrieve mistreat

aggrieved unjustly injured

aghast horrified

agile nimble

agitate stir up

agnate related on the father's side

agnostic not knowing whether God exists

agrarian pertaining to farming

agronomy science of crop production

air discuss, broadcast

airs pretension

akimbo with hands on hips

akin related

al fresco outdoors

alacrity swiftness

albatross large sea bird

albino lacking pigmentation

alcove recess, niche

alias assumed name

alibi excuse

alienate estrange, antagonize

alight land, descend, to happen to find a place to rest

allay to reassure

allege assert without proof

allegiance loyalty

allegory fable

allegro fast

alleviate lessen, assuage

alliteration repetition of the same sound

allocate distribute

allot allocate, ration

allude refer to indirectly

ally unite for a purpose

almanac calendar with additional information

alms charity

aloof arrogant, detached

altercation argument

altitude height

alto low female voice

altruism benevolence, generosity

amalgamation mixture

amass collect

ambient surrounding, environment

ambiguous unclear

ambivalence conflicting emotions

ambulatory able to walk

ameliorate improve

amenable agreeable

amend correct

amenities courtesies, comforts

amenity pleasantness

amiable friendly

amid among

amiss wrong, out of place

amity friendship, good will

amnesty pardon

amoral without morals

amorous loving, sexual

amorphous shapeless

amortize pay by installments

amphibious able to operate in water and land

amphitheater oval-shaped theater

amuck murderous frenzy

amulet charm, talisman

amuse entertain

anachronistic out of historical order

anaerobic without oxygen

anagram a word formed by rearranging the letters of another word

analgesic pain-soother

Quiz 2 (Antonyms)

Directions: Choose the word most opposite in meaning to the capitalized word. Answers are on page 100.

1. GRATUITOUS: (A) voluntary   (B) arduous   (C) solicitous
                  (D) righteous   (E) befitting

2. FALLOW: (A) fatuous   (B) productive   (C) bountiful
              (D) pertinacious   (E) opprobrious

3. METTLE: (A) ad hoc   (B) perdition   (C) woe
              (D) trepidation   (E) apathy

4. SAVANT: (A) dolt   (B) sage   (C) attaché
              (D) apropos comment   (E) state of confusion

5. RIFE: (A) multitudinous   (B) blemished   (C) sturdy
            (D) counterfeit   (E) sparse

6. ABRIDGE: (A) distend   (B) assail   (C) unfetter
               (D) enfeeble   (E) prove

7. PRODIGAL: (A) bountiful   (B) dependent   (C) provident
                (D) superfluous   (E) profligate

8. REQUIEM: (A) humility   (B) prerequisite   (C) resolution
               (D) reign   (E) hiatus

9. METE: (A) indict   (B) convoke   (C) hamper
            (D) disseminate   (E) deviate

10. SEVERANCE: (A) continuation   (B) dichotomy
                 (C) astringency   (D) disclosure
                 (E) remonstrance

analogous similar

analogy point-by-point comparison

anarchist terrorist, nihilist

anarchy absence of government, chaos

anathema curse, abomination

anecdote story

aneurysm bulging in a blood vessel

angst anxiety, dread

animadversion critical remark

12

animated exuberant

animosity dislike

animus hate

annals historical records

annex to attach, to take possession of

annihilate destroy

annotate to add explanatory notes

annul cancel

annular ring-shaped

anodyne pain soothing

anoint consecrate, apply ointment

anomalous abnormal

anonymity state of being anonymous

antagonistic hostile

antagonize harass

antechamber waiting room

antediluvian ancient, obsolete

anthology collection

anthrax disease, bacterium

antic caper, prank

antipathy repulsion, hated

antipodal exactly opposite

antiquated outdated, obsolete

antiquity ancient times

antithesis direct opposite

apartheid racial segregation

apathetic unconcerned, uninterested

apathy indifference

ape mimic

aperture opening

apex highest point

aphasia speechless

aphorism maxim

aplomb poise

apocalyptic ominous, doomed

apocryphal of doubtful authenticity

apoplexy stroke

apostate one who abandons one's faith

apotheosis deification

appall horrify

apparition phantom

appease pacify

appellation title

append affix

apposite apt

apprehensive anxious, worried

apprise inform

approbation approval

apropos appropriate

apt suitable

aptitude ability

aquatic pertaining to water

arbiter judge

arbitrament final judgment

arbitrary tyrannical, capricious

arcane secret, difficult to understand

archaic antiquated

archetype original model, epitome

archipelago group of island

archives public records

ardent passionate

ardor passion
arduous hard
Argonauts gold-seekers, adventurers
argot specialized vocabulary, jargon
aria operatic song
arid dry, dull
aristocrat nobleman
armada fleet of ships
armistice truce
arraign indict
array arrangement
arrears in debt
arrogate seize without right
arroyo gully
arsenal supply, stockpile of weapons
artful skillful, cunning
articulate well-spoken
artifice trick
artless naive, simple
ascend rise
ascendancy powerful state
ascertain discover
ascetic self-denying
ascribe to attribute
aseptic sterile
ashen pale
asinine stupid
askance to view with suspicion
askew crooked
aspersion slander
asphyxiate suffocate

aspirant contestant
aspiration ambition
assail attack
assassin murderer
assent agree
assert affirm
assess appraise
assiduous hard-working
assimilate absorb, integrate
assonance partial rhyme
assuage lessen (pain)
astral pertaining to stars
astringent causing contraction, severe
astute wise
asunder apart, into separate parts
asylum place of refuge
asymmetric uneven
atavistic exhibiting the characteristics of one's forebears
atelier workshop
atoll reef
atomize vaporize
atone make amends
atrophy the wasting away of muscle
attenuate weaken, assuage
attest testify
attire dress
attribute ascribe
attrition deterioration, reduction

Quiz 3 (Matching)

Match each word in the first column with its definition in the second column. Answers are on page 100.

1.	ANATHEMA	A.	hard
2.	ANNIHILATE	B.	curse
3.	ANOMALOUS	C.	gully
4.	APATHETIC	D.	suffocate
5.	ARCHAIC	E.	antiquated
6.	ARDUOUS	F.	destroy
7.	ARROYO	G.	abnormal
8.	ASPHYXIATE	H.	unconcerned
9.	ASTRINGENT	I.	make amends
10.	ATONE	J.	causing contraction

atypical abnormal

au courant well informed, chic

audacity boldness

audient listening, attentive

audition tryout

augment increase, supplement

augur predict

august noble, majestic

aura atmosphere, emanation

auspices patronage, protection

auspicious favorable

austere harsh, Spartan

authorize grant, sanction

automaton robot

autonomous self-governing

auxiliary secondary, supportive

avail assistance

avant-garde vanguard

avarice greed

avatar incarnation

averse loath, reluctant

avert turn away

avian pertaining to birds

avid enthusiastic

avocation hobby

avouch attest, guarantee

avow declare

avuncular like an uncle

awry crooked

axiom self-evident truth

aye affirmative vote

azure sky blue

B

babbittry smugness

bacchanal orgy, drunken celebration

badger pester

badinage banter

bagatelle nonentity, trifle

bailiwick area of concern or business

15

baleen whalebone

baleful hostile, malignant

balk hesitate

balky hesitant

ballad song

ballast counterbalance

ballistics study of projectiles

balm soothing ointment

banal trite

bandy exchange

bane poison, nuisance

barbarian savage

bard poet

baroque ornate

barrister lawyer

bask take pleasure in, sun

basso low male voice

bastion fort

bathos sentimentality

batten fasten, board up

battery physical attack

bauble trinket

beatify sanctify

beatitude state of bliss

beckon lure

becoming proper

bedlam uproar

befit to be suitable

beget produce, procreate

begrudge resent, envy

beguile deceive, seduce

behemoth monster

behest command

beholden in debt, obliged

belabor assail verbally, dwell on

belated delayed, overdue

beleaguer besiege

belfry bell tower

belie misrepresent, disprove

belittle disparage

bellicose warlike

belligerent combative

bellow shout

bellwether leader, guide

bemoan lament

bemused bewildered

benchmark standard

benediction blessing

benefactor patron

benevolent kind

benign harmless

bent determined

bequeath will

bequest gift, endowment

berate scold

bereave to rob, to deprive somebody of a love one, especially through death

---

Quiz 4 (Antonyms)

<u>Directions:</u> Choose the word most opposite in meaning to the capitalized word. Answers are on page 100.

1. HYPOCRITICAL: (A) forthright (B) judicious
    (C) circumspect (D) puritanical
    (E) unorthodox

2. VOLUMINOUS: (A) obscure (B) cantankerous
    (C) unsubstantial (D) tenacious
    (E) opprobrious

3. FANATICISM: (A) delusion (B) fascism (C) remorse
    (D) cynicism (E) indifference

4. INTERMINABLE: (A) finite (B) jejune (C) tranquil
    (D) incessant (E) imprudent

5. ORNATE: (A) Spartan (B) blemished (C) sturdy
    (D) counterfeit (E) temporary

6. MUTABILITY: (A) simplicity (B) apprehension
    (C) frailty (D) maverick (E) tenacity

7. VIRULENT: (A) benign (B) intrepid (C) malignant
    (D) hyperbolic (E) tentative

8. ABSTEMIOUS: (A) timely (B) immoderate
    (C) bellicose (D) servile (E) irreligious

9. VERBOSE: (A) subliminal (B) myopic (C) pithy
    (D) dauntless (E) ubiquitous

10. VISCID: (A) subtle (B) faint (C) slick (D) vicious
    (E) difficult

---

bereft deprived of

berserk crazed with anger

beseech implore, beg

beset harass, encircle

besiege beleaguer, surround

besmirch slander, sully

bespeak attest

bestial beast-like, brutal

bestow offer, grant

betrothed engaged

17

bevy group
bibliography list of sources of information
bicameral having two legislative branches
bicker quarrel
biennial occurring every two years
bilateral two-sided
bilious ill-tempered
bilk swindle
biodegradable naturally decaying
biopsy removing tissue for examination
biped two-footed animal
bistro tavern, cafe
bivouac encampment
blandish flatter, grovel
blasé bored with life
blasphemy insulting God
bleak cheerless, forlorn
blight decay
bliss happiness
blithe joyous
bloated swollen
bode portend
bogus forged, false
bogy bugbear
boisterous noisy
bolt move quickly and suddenly
bombast pompous speech
bon vivant gourmet, epicure

bona fide made in good faith
bonanza a stroke of luck
boon payoff, windfall
boor vulgar person
bootless unavailing
booty loot, stolen goods
botch bungle
bourgeois middle class
bovine cow-like
boycott abstain in protest
bracing refreshing
brackish salty
brandish display menacingly
bravado feigned bravery
bravura technically difficult, brilliant
brawn strength
brevity shortness of expression
brigand robber
brink edge, threshold
broach bring up a topic for conversation
bromide cliché
brook tolerate
browbeat to bully
brusque curt
bucolic rustic
buffet blow, pummel
buffoon fool, joker
bulwark fortification
buncombe empty, showy talk
buoyant floatable, cheerful
burgeon sprout

burlesque farce
burly husky
buttress support

C

cabal a group of conspirators
cabaret nightclub
cache hiding place
cachet prestige
cacophony dissonance, harsh noise
cadaver corpse
cadaverous haggard
cadence rhythm
cadet a student of a military academy
cadge beg
cadre small group
cajole encourage, coax
calamity disaster
calculating scheming
caliber ability, character
callous insensitive
callow inexperienced
calumny slander
camaraderie fellowship
canaille rabble
canard hoax
candid frank, unrehearsed
candor frankness
canine pertaining to dogs

canon rule
cant insincere speech
cantankerous peevish
cantata musical composition
canvass survey
capacious spacious
capillary thin tube
capital most significant, pertaining to wealth
capitol legislative building
capitulate surrender
capricious fickle, impulsive
caption title
captious fond of finding fault in others
captivate engross, fascinate
carafe bottle
carbine rifle
carcinogenic causing cancer
carcinoma tumor
cardinal chief
cardiologist one who studies the heart
careen swerve
carrion decaying flesh
cartographer mapmaker
cascade waterfall
cashmere fine wool from Asia
Cassandra unheeded prophet
castigate criticize
castrate remove the testicles

Quiz 5 (Matching)

Match each word in the first column with its definition in the second column. Answers are on page 100.

1.	BESMIRCH	A.	unheeded prophet
2.	BICAMERAL	B.	peevish
3.	BILATERAL	C.	pertaining to dogs
4.	BOOTLESS	D.	plot
5.	BRANDISH	E.	farce
6.	BURLESQUE	F.	display menacingly
7.	CABAL	G.	unavailing
8.	CANINE	H.	two-sided
9.	CANTANKEROUS	I.	having two legislative branches
10.	CASSANDRA	J.	sully

casuistry specious reasoning

cataclysm catastrophe

catastrophic disastrous

categorical absolute, certain

cathartic purgative, purifying

catholic universal, worldly

caucus meeting

cause célèbre celebrated legal case

caustic scathing (of speech)

cauterize to sear

cavalier disdainful, nonchalant

caveat warning

caveat emptor buyer beware

cavil quibble

cavort frolic

cede transfer ownership, relinquish

celestial heavenly

celibate abstaining from sex

cenotaph empty tomb, monument

censorious condemning speech

censure condemn

ceramics pottery

cerebral pertaining to the brain

cessation a stopping

chafe abrade

chagrin embarrassment

chalice goblet

champion defend

chaperon escort

charade pantomime, sham

charlatan quack, imposter

chartreuse greenish yellow

chary cautious

chaste pure, virgin

chasten castigate

chateau castle

cheeky brass, forward

cherub cupid

cherubic sweet, innocent

chicanery trickery

chide scold

chimerical imaginary, dreamlike

choleric easily angered

chortle laugh, snort

chronic continual (usually of illness)

chronicle a history, record

chronology arrangement by time

churl a boor

chutzpah gall

Cimmerian dim, unlit

cipher zero, nobody, a code

circa about (of time)

circuitous roundabout

circumcise remove the foreskin

circumlocution roundabout expression

circumspect cautious

circumvent evade, thwart

citadel fortress

citation summons to appear in court

clamor noise

clan extended family

clandestine secret

claustrophobia fear of enclosed places

cleave split

cleft split

clemency forgiveness

clique a small group

cloister refuge, monastery

clone duplicate

clout influence

cloven split

cloy glut, to sicken by excess

cloyed jaded

co-opt preempt, usurp

coagulate thicken

coalesce combine

coda concluding passage

coddle pamper

codicil supplement to a will

coercion force

coffer strongbox

cogent well-put, convincing

cogitate ponder

cognate from the same source

cognizant aware, mindful

cognomen family name

cohabit live together

cohere stick together

cohort an associate

coiffure hairdo

collaborate work together

collar seize, arrest

collateral securities for a debt

colloquial informal speech

colloquy conference

collusion conspiracy

colonnade row of columns

Quiz 6 (Antonyms)

Directions: Choose the word most opposite in meaning to the capitalized word. Answers are on page 100.

1. DERISION: (A) urgency   (B) admonishment
                  (C) uniqueness   (D) diversity   (E) acclaim

2. ANTIPATHY: (A) fondness   (B) disagreement
                  (C) boorishness   (D) provocation
                  (E) opprobrium

3. CAJOLE: (A) implore   (B) glance at   (C) belittle
                  (D) ennoble   (E) engender

4. CENSURE: (A) prevaricate   (B) titillate   (C) aggrandize
                  (D) obscure   (E) sanction

5. ADULATION: (A) immutability   (B) reluctance
                  (C) reflection   (D) defamation
                  (E) indifference

6. NOISOME: (A) salubrious   (B) affable   (C) multifarious
                  (D) provident   (E) officious

7. CONSECRATE: (A) curb   (B) destroy   (C) curse
                  (D) inveigh   (E) exculpate

8. ILLUSTRIOUS: (A) bellicose   (B) ignoble   (C) theoretical
                  (D) esoteric   (E) immaculate

9. DEIGN: (A) inveigh   (B) gainsay   (C) speculate   (D) reject
                  (E) laud

10. SUBTERFUGE: (A) bewilderment   (B) artlessness   (C) deceit
                  (D) felicitation   (E) jeopardy

---

comatose stupor

combine unite, blend

commandeer seize for military use

commemorate observe

commend praise

commensurate proportionate

commiserate empathize

commissary food store

commission authorization to
perform a task
commodious spacious
commodity product
commodore naval officer
communion fellowship
commutation exchange,
substitution
commute lessen punishment
compact covenant
compassion kindness
compatible well-matched,
harmonious
compatriot countryman
compelling convincing,
persuasive
compendium summary
compensate make up for
compensatory redeeming
competence skillfulness
compile collect
complacent self-satisfied,
oblivious to coming danger
compliant submissive,
conforming
complicity guilt by association
comport to conduct oneself
composed cool, self-possessed
compound augment
comprehensive thorough
comprise consist of
compulsive obsessive
compulsory obligatory
compunction remorse
concatenate link

concave curving inward
concede yield, grant
concerted done together,
intensive effort
conch spiral shell
conciliatory reconciling,
restoring goodwill
concise brief
conclusive convincing, ending
doubt
concoct devise
concomitant accompanying,
concurrent
concord accord
concordat agreement
concourse throng, open space
for a gathering
concubine mistress
concur agree
concurrent simultaneous
condescend patronize, talk
down to
condiment seasoning
condolence commiseration
condone overlook wrong doing,
pardon
conducive helping
conduit pipe
confabulate discuss, give a
fictitious account of a past event
confection candy
confederacy alliance
confer bestow
conference meeting
confidant trusted friend

23

confide trust another (with secrets)

confiscate seize

conflagration large fire

confluence flowing together

confound bewilder

confront challenge

confuse perplex

confute disprove

congeal solidify

congenial friendly

congenital inborn, existing from birth

congeries pile

congruence conformity

coniferous bearing cones

conjecture hypothesis, speculation

conjugal pertaining to marriage

conjure summon

connive conspire

connoisseur an expert, gourmet

consanguineous related by blood

conscientious honorable, upright

conscription draft, enlistment

consecrate make holy

consecutive one after another

consensus general agreement

considered well thought-out, contemplated

consign assign

consolation comfort, solace

console comfort

consolidate unite, strengthen

consonant harmonious

consort spouse

consortium cartel

conspicuous obvious

conspire plot

constellation arrangement of stars

consternation anxiety, bewilderment

constrained confined

construe interpret

consummate perfect

contagion infectious agent

contemplate meditate

contempt disdain

contend struggle

contented satisfied

contentious argumentative

contiguous adjacent, abutting

continence self-control

contingent conditional

contort twist

contraband illicit goods

contraction shrinkage

contractual related to a contract

contrariety opposition

contrast difference, comparison

contravene oppose

contretemps unfortunate occurrence

contrite apologetic

contrive arrange, artificial

controversial subject to dispute

controvert dispute

contumacy disobedience

contusion bruise

Quiz 7 (Matching)

Match each word in the first column with its definition in the second column. Answers are on page 100.

1.	COMMANDEER	A.	seize for military use
2.	COMMUNION	B.	apologetic
3.	COMPATRIOT	C.	perfect
4.	CONCERTED	D.	accord
5.	CONCORD	E.	done together
6.	CONFLUENCE	F.	pile
7.	CONGERIES	G.	flowing together
8.	CONSONANT	H.	harmonious
9.	CONSUMMATE	I.	countryman
10.	CONTRITE	J.	fellowship

---

conundrum puzzle, enigma

convene assemble (a group)

conventional customary, standard

converge come together

conversant familiar

converse opposite

convex curving outward

convey communicate

conviction strongly held belief

convivial sociable, festive

convocation gathering

convoke convene, summon

convoluted twisted, complicated

copious abundant

coquette a flirt

cordial friendly

cordon bond, chain, barrier

cornucopia cone-shaped horn filled with fruit

corollary consequence

coronation crowning of a sovereign

corporeal of the body

corps group of people

corpulent fat

corroborate confirm

cortege procession

coruscate sparkle

cosmopolitan worldly, sophisticated

cosset coddle

coterie small group

countenance facial expression

countermand overrule

counterstrike strike back

countervail counterbalance

coup masterstroke, sudden takeover

coup de grâce final stroke, a blow of mercy

court-martial military trial

courtesan prostitute

courtier member of the king's court

covenant agreement, pact

covert secret

covet desire

cower showing fear

crass crude

crave desire

craven cowardly

credence belief

credenza buffet

credulity gullibility

credulous believing

creed belief

crescendo becoming louder

crestfallen dejected

crevice crack

cringe cower

criterion a standard used in judging

critique examination, criticism

croon sing

cruet bottle

crux gist, key

cryptic mysterious, puzzling

cubism a style of painting

cudgel club

culinary pertaining to cooking

cull pick out, select

culminate climax

culpable blameworthy

culprit offender

culvert drain

cumbersome unwieldy

cumulative accumulate

cupidity greed

curb restrain, block

curmudgeon boor, bad-tempered

curriculum course of study

curry seek favor by flattery

cursory hasty

curt abrupt, rude

curtail shorten

cyclone storm

cynical scornful of the motives or sincerity of others

cynosure celebrity, center of attention

czar Russian emperor

D

dab touch lightly

dais platform

dally procrastinate, linger

dank cold and damp

dauntless courageous

de facto actual, in effect

de jure legally

de rigueur very formal, compulsory

deadpan expressionless

dearth scarcity

debacle a rout, defeat

debase degrade

debauch corrupt

Quiz 8 (Antonyms)

<u>Directions:</u> Choose the word most opposite in meaning to the capitalized word. Answers are on page 100.

1. UPSHOT: (A) consequence (B) descent (C) annihilation
   (D) termination (E) inception

2. WHET: (A) obscure (B) blunt (C) desiccate
   (D) imbibe (E) enervate

3. PRODIGY: (A) vacuous comment (B) hegemony (C) plane
   (D) common occurrence (E) capitulation

4. AMBULATORY: (A) immutable (B) obdurate
   (C) hospitalized (D) pedantic
   (E) stationary

5. PLATITUDE: (A) sincere comment (B) enigmatic comment
   (C) hostile comment
   (D) disingenuous comment
   (E) original comment

6. SEEMLY: (A) redoubtable (B) flaccid (C) imperceptible
   (D) indigenous (E) unbecoming

7. CHAMPION: (A) relinquish (B) contest (C) oppress
   (D) modify (E) withhold

8. AIR: (A) release (B) differ (C) expose
   (D) betray (E) enshroud

9. PERTURBATION: (A) impotence (B) obstruction
   (C) prediction (D) equanimity
   (E) chivalry

10: TEMPESTUOUS: (A) prodigal (B) reticent (C) serene
    (D) phenomenal (E) accountable

---

debauchery indulgence

debilitate weaken

debonair sophisticated, affable

debrief interrogate, inform

debunk refute, expose

debutante a girl debuting into society

27

decadence decay (e.g. moral or cultural)

decant pour

decapitate kill by beheading

decathlon athletic contest

deceive trick

deciduous shedding leaves

decimate destroy

decipher decode

decline decrease in number

decommission take a ship out of service

decorous seemly, dignified

decorum protocol, etiquette

decree official order

decrepitude enfeeblement

decry castigate

deduce conclude

deduct subtract

deem judge

deface mar, disfigure

defamation (noun) slander

defame (verb) slander

defeatist one who is resigned to defeat

defer postpone

deference courteously yielding to another

deficit shortage

defile pollute, corrupt

definitive conclusive, final

deflect turn aside

deflower despoil

defraud swindle

defray pay

deft skillful

defunct extinct

degrade demean

dehydrate dry out

deign condescend

deity a god

delectable delicious

delegate authorize

delete remove

deleterious harmful

deliberate ponder

delineate draw a line around, describe

delinquent negligent, culpable

delirium mental confusion, ecstasy

delude deceive

deluge a flood

delve dig, explore (of ideas)

demagogue a politician who appeals to base instincts

demean degrade

demeanor behavior

demented deranged

demise death

demobilize disband

demography study of human populations

demoralize dishearten

demote lower in rank

demur take (mild) exception, balk

demure sedate, reserved

denigrate defame

denizen dweller

28

denomination class, sect

denote signify, stand for

denouement resolution

denounce condemn

denude strip bare

depart leave

depict portray

deplete exhaust

deplore condemn

deploy arrange forces

deportment behavior, posture

deposition testimony

depravity immorality, wickedness

deprecate belittle

depredation preying on, plunder

deprive take away

deracinate uproot

derelict negligent

deride ridicule

derisive mocking

derogatory degrading

derrick crane

desecrate profane, defile

desiccate dehydrate

designate appoint

desist stop

desolate forsaken

despicable contemptible

despise loathe

despondent depressed

despot tyrant

destitute poor

desuetude disuse

desultory without direction in life

detached emotionally removed

detain confine

détente truce

detention confinement

deter discourage, prevent

deterrent hindrance, disincentive

detract lessen, undermine

detractor one who criticizes

detrimental harmful

detritus debris

devastate lay waste

deviate turn away from

devise plan

devoid empty

devotee enthusiast, follower

devout pious

diabolical devilish

dialectic pertaining to debate

diaphanous sheer, translucent

diatribe long denunciation

dicey risky

dichotomy a division into two parts

dictate command

dictum saying

didactic instructional

diffident shy

digress ramble

29

Quiz 9 (Matching)

Match each word in the first column with its definition in the second column. Answers are on page 100.

1.	DEBUNK	A.	decode
2.	DECIPHER	B.	refute
3.	DEDUCE	C.	conclusive
4.	DEFINITIVE	D.	conclude
5.	DEFUNCT	E.	to draw a line around
6.	DELINEATE	F.	extinct
7.	DENOMINATION	G.	belittle
8.	DEPRECATE	H.	sect
9.	DESOLATE	I.	pertaining to debate
10.	DIALECTIC	J.	forsaken

---

dilapidated neglected

dilate enlarge

dilatory procrastinating

dilemma a difficult choice

dilettante amateur, dabbler

diligent hard-working

diminution reduction

diocese district

dire dreadful

dirigible airship, blimp

disabuse correct

disaffect alienate

disarray disorder

disavow deny, disown

disband disperse

disburse pay out

discernible visible

discerning observant

disclaim renounce

disconcert confuse

disconsolate inconsolable

discord lack of harmony

discourse conversation

discreet prudent

discrepancy difference, disagreement

discrete separate

discretion prudence, the ability to make well-reasoned decisions

discriminating able to see differences

discursive rambling

disdain contempt

disengage release, detach

disfigure mar, ruin

disgruntled disappointed

dishevel muss

disinclination unwillingness

disingenuous deceptive, insincere

disinter unearth

disinterested impartial

disjointed disconnected, incoherent

dismal gloomy

dismantle take apart

dismay dread

disparage belittle

disparate various

disparity difference, inequality

dispassionate impartial

dispatch send

dispel cause to banish

disperse scatter

dispirit discourage

disposition attitude, temper

dispossess take away possessions

disputatious fond of arguing

dispute debate

disquietude anxiety

disquisition elaborate treatise

disrepute disgrace

dissemble pretend, hide true beliefs

disseminate distribute

dissent disagree with the majority

dissertation lecture

dissidence disagreement

dissipate scatter, squander

dissolute profligate, immoral

dissolution disintegration

dissonance discord

dissuade deter

distend swell

distortion misinterpret, lie

distract divert

distrait preoccupied, absent-minded

distraught distressed

distrust suspect

dither move without purpose

diurnal daily

diva prima donna

diverge branch off

diverse varying

diversion pastime

diversity variety

divest strip, deprive

dividend distributed profits

divine foretell

divisive causing conflict

divulge disclose

docile domesticated, trained

dock curtail

doctrinaire dogmatic

document verify

dodder tremble

dogged persistent

doggerel poor verse

dogmatic certain, unchanging in opinion

dolce sweetly and gently

doldrums dullness

doleful sorrowful

Quiz 10 (Antonyms)

<u>Directions:</u> Choose the word most opposite in meaning to the capitalized word. Answers are on page 100.

1. CURB: (A) bridle (B) encourage (C) reproach (D) ameliorate (E) perjure

2. DOCUMENT: (A) copy (B) implement (C) gainsay (D) blanch (E) rant

3. FLUID: (A) radiant (B) smooth (C) solid (D) balky (E) craggy

4. BOLT: (A) linger (B) refrain from (C) subdue (D) strip (E) transgress

5. TABLE: (A) palliate (B) acclimate (C) garner (D) propound (E) expedite

6. HARBOR: (A) provide shelter (B) banish (C) acquiesce (D) extol (E) capitulate

7. DISREPUTE: (A) impertinence (B) indifference (C) honor (D) affluence (E) apathy

8. STEEP: (A) desiccate (B) intensify (C) pontificate (D) whet (E) hamper

9. RENT: (A) reserved (B) restored (C) razed (D) busy (E) kinetic

10. EXACT: (A) extract (B) starve (C) lecture (D) menace (E) condone

dolorous gloomy
domicile home
dominion area of authority
don assume, put on
donor contributor
dormant asleep
dossier file
dotage senility
doting attending

double-entendre having two meanings one of which is sexually suggestive
doughty resolute, unafraid
dour sullen
dowager widow
doyen dean of a group
draconian harsh
dregs residue, riffraff
drivel inane speech

32

droll amusing

drone speak in a monotonic voice

dubious doubtful

ductile stretchable

dudgeon resentment, indignant humor

duenna governess

duet twosome

dulcet melodious

dupe one who is easily trick, victim

duplicity deceit, treachery

duress coercion

dynamic energetic

E

ebb recede

ebullient exuberant

eccentric odd, weird

ecclesiastical churchly

echelon degree, rank

éclat brilliance

eclectic from many sources

ectoderm top layer of skin

ecumenical universal, promoting unity

edict order

edifice building

edify instruct

editorialize express an opinion

educe draw forth, evoke

efface obliterate

effeminate unmanly

effervescence exuberance

effete worn out

efficacious effective

efficacy effectiveness

effigy likeness, mannequin

effloresce to bloom

effrontery insolence

effulgent brilliant

effusion pouring forth

egocentric self-centered

egregious grossly wrong

egress exit

ejaculate exclaim

eke supplement with great effort, strain

elaboration detailed explanation

elate raise spirits

electorate voters

eleemosynary pertaining to charity

elegant refined, exquisite

elegiac sad

elephantine large

elicit provoke

elide omit

elite upper-class

ellipsis omission of words

eloquent well-spoken

elucidate make clear, explain

elude evade

elusive evasive

emaciated underfed, gaunt

emancipate liberate

emasculate castrate, dispirit

embargo restriction

embellish exaggerate, adorn

embezzlement theft

emblazon imprint, brand

embody personify

embrace accept, adopt

embrangle embroil

embroil involve with trouble

embryonic rudimentary, nascent

emend correct

emergent appearing

emeritus retired, but retaining title

eminent distinguished, famous

emissary messenger

emote to display exaggerated emotion

empathy compassion, sympathy

employ make use of

empower enable, grant

emulate imitate

enact decree, ordain

enamored charmed, captivated

enate related on the mother's side

encapsulate condense

enchant charm

enclave area enclosed within another region

encomium praise

encompass contain, encircle

encore additional performance

encroach trespass

encumber burden

encyclopedic comprehensive

endear enamor

endeavor attempt, strive

endemic peculiar to a particular region

endocrinologist one who studies glands of internal secretion

endoderm within the skin

endorse approve

endowment property, gift

endure to suffer without giving up

enervate weaken

enfranchise liberate, grant the right to vote

engaging enchanting, charming

engender generate, prompt

engrave carve into a material

engross captivate

engulf overwhelm

enhance improve

enigmatic puzzling

enjoin urge, order, forbid

enlighten inform

enlist join

enmity hostility, hatred

ennoble exalt

ennui boredom, world-weariness

Quiz 11 (Matching)

Match each word in the first column with its definition in the second column. Answers are on page 100.

1.	DORMANT	A.	exuberant
2.	DOUGHTY	B.	puzzling
3.	DUET	C.	comprehensive
4.	EBULLIENT	D.	asleep
5.	EFFEMINATE	E.	omission of words
6.	ELLIPSIS	F.	unmanly
7.	EMANCIPATE	G.	charm
8.	ENCHANT	H.	liberate
9.	ENCYCLOPEDIC	I.	twosome
10.	ENIGMATIC	J.	resolute

enormity large, tragic

ensemble musical group

enshroud cover, obscure

ensnare trap, lure

ensue follow immediately

entail involve, necessitate

enterprise undertaking

enthrall mesmerize

entice lure

entomology the study of insects

entourage assemblage, staff

entreat plead

entrench fortify

entrepreneur businessman

enumerate count

enviable desirable

envision imagine, visualize

envoy messenger

eon long period of time

ephemeral short-lived

epic majestic, a long narrative poem

epicure gourmet

epidemic spreading rapidly

epidemiology study of the spread of disease

epigram saying

episode incident

epistemology the branch of philosophy dealing with knowledge

epithet name, appellation

epoch era

epoxy glue

equable even-tempered

equanimity composure, poise

equine pertaining to horses

equitable fair

equivocate make intentionally ambiguous

era period of time

eradicate abolish

ergo therefore

erode wear away

35

err mistake, misjudge

errant wandering

erratic constantly changing

erroneous mistaken

ersatz artificial

erudite learned

erupt burst forth

escalate intensify

escapade adventure

escarpment a steep slope

eschew avoid

esoteric known by only a few

esplanade boardwalk

espouse advocate

esteem respect

esthetic artistic

estimable meritorious

estrange alienate

eternal endless

ethereal light, airy

ethical conforming to accepted standards of behavior

ethos beliefs of a group

etiquette manners

etymology study of words

euphemism genteel expression

euphoria elation

euthanasia mercy-killing

evade avoid

evanescent fleeting, very brief

evangelical proselytizing

evasive elusive

eventful momentous

eventual ultimate, coming

eventuate bring about

evidential pertaining to evidence

evince attest, demonstrate

eviscerate disembowel

evoke draw forth

evolution gradual change

ewe female sheep

ex officio by virtue of position

exacerbate worsen

exact use authority to force payment

exacting demanding, difficult

exalt glorify

exasperate irritate

excerpt selection, extract

excision removal

exclaim shout

exclude shut out

exclusive prohibitive

excommunicate expel

excruciate torture

execrable abominable

execute put into effect

exegesis interpretation

Quiz 12 (Antonyms)

Directions: Choose the word most opposite in meaning to the capitalized word. Answers are on page 100.

1. DISCORD: (A) agreement   (B) supposition   (C) strife
   (D) scrutiny   (E) antithesis

2. KEEN: (A) concentrated   (B) languid   (C) rash
   (D) caustic   (E) voracious

3. IRRELEVANT: (A) moot   (B) onerous   (C) impertinent
   (D) germane   (E) true

4. FACILITATE: (A) appease   (B) expedite   (C) extol
   (D) foil   (E) precipitate

5. FEND: (A) absorb   (B) disperse   (C) intensify
   (D) reflect   (E) halt

6. PORTLY: (A) ill   (B) thin   (C) dull
   (D) rotund   (E) insipid

7. DEPLETE: (A) tax   (B) annotate   (C) replenish
   (D) lecture   (E) vanquish

8. INCESSANT: (A) intermittent (B) continual (C) increasing
   (D) enclosing   (E) expanding

9. PERJURE: (A) absolve   (B) forswear   (C) impeach
   (D) authenticate   (E) mortify

10. PLETHORA: (A) dishonor   (B) paucity   (C) glut
    (D) resolve   (E) deluge

exemplary outstanding

exempt excuse

exhaustive thorough

exhibitionist one who draws attention to himself

exhort strongly urge

exhume uncover

exigency urgency

exiguous scanty

exile banish

exodus departure, migration

exonerate free from blame

37

exorbitant expensive

exorcise expel

expanse extent of land

expansive sweeping

expedient advantageous

expedite hasten

expel drive out

expertise knowledge, ability

expiate atone

expletive curse, invective

expliate atone

explicate explain

explicit definite, clear

exploit utilize, milk

expose divulge, reveal

expostulate protest

expound explain

expropriate dispossess, confiscate

expunge erase

exquisite beautifully made

extant existing

extemporize improvise

extent scope

extenuate mitigate

extirpate seek out and destroy

extol praise highly

extort obtain under duress

extract to pull out, exact

extradite deport, deliver

extraneous not essential

extrapolate infer

extremity farthest point, boundary

extricate disentangle

extroverted outgoing

extrude force out

exuberant joyous

exude emit

exult rejoice

F

fabrication a lie

facade mask, front of a building

facet aspect

facetious joking, sarcastic

facile easy

facilitate make easier

facility skill

facsimile duplicate

faction clique, sect

factious causing disagreement

factitious artificial

factotum handyman

fallacious false

fallacy false belief

fallow unproductive, unplowed

falsetto high male voice

falter waver

fanaticism excessive zeal

fane temple

fanfare publicity

farcical absurd, ridiculous

farrago mixture

fascism totalitarianism, extreme nationalism

fastidious meticulous

fatal resulting in death

fathom understand

fatuity foolishness

fatuous inane, stupid

fauna animals

faux pas false step, mistake

fealty loyalty

feasible likely to succeed

feat deed, remarkable achievement

febrile feverish, delirious

feckless incompetent

fecund fertile

feign pretend

felicity happiness

felonious criminal

femme fatale a woman who leads men to their destruction

fend ward off

feral untamed, wild

ferment turmoil

ferret rummage through

fertile fruitful

fervor intensity

fester decay, to make someone increasingly bitter

festive joyous

festoon decorate

fete to honor with an event

fetid stinking

fetters shackles

fey eccentric, whimsical

fiasco debacle

fiat decree

fickle always changing one's mind

fictitious invented, imaginary

fidelity loyalty

figment falsehood, fantasy

filch steal

filial son

filibuster long speech

fillip stimulus

finale conclusion

finesse skill

firebrand agitator

firmament sky

fiscal monetary

fitful starting and stopping irregularly

fjord coastal inlet

flabbergasted amazed, dumbfounded

flagellate whip

flagrant outrageous, blatant

flail whip, to thrash something around uncontrollably and menacingly

fledgling just beginning, struggling

flippant pert, glib, dismissive

florid ruddy, ornate

Quiz 13 (Matching)

Match each word in the first column with its definition in the second column. Answers are on page 100.

1.	EXHORT	A.	free from blame
2.	EXONERATE	B.	strongly urge
3.	EXPOSTULATE	C.	agitator
4.	EXTRADITE	D.	untamed
5.	EXULT	E.	debacle
6.	FACTITIOUS	F.	inane
7.	FATUOUS	G.	artificial
8.	FERAL	H.	deport
9.	FIASCO	I.	rejoice
10.	FIREBRAND	J.	protest

---

flout to show disregard for the law or rules

fluctuate waver, vary

foible weakness, minor fault

foil defeat, thwart

foist palm off a fake

foment instigate

font source, fountainhead, set of type

forage search for food

foray raid

forbear abstain, restrain oneself

force majeure superior force

foreboding ominous

foreclose exclude

forensic pertaining to debate

foresight ability to predict the future

forestall thwart, preempt

forgo relinquish (usually voluntarily)

forsake abandon

forswear deny

forthright frank

forthwith immediately

fortify strengthen

fortitude resilience, courage

fortuitous lucky

foster encourage, cultivate

founder sink. fail

fracas noisy fight

fragile easily broken

fragmented broken into fragments

fraternity brotherhood

fraught filled

frenetic harried, neurotic

fret worry

fritter squander

frivolity playfulness

frolic romp, play

frond bending tree

frugal thrifty

fruitful productive

fruition realization, completion

fruitless unprofitable, barren

fulminate denounce, menace

fulsome excessive, insincere

fuming angry

furlough leave of absence

furor commotion

furtive stealthy

fusillade bombardment

futile hopeless

G

gaffe embarrassing mistake

gainful profitable

gainsay contradict

galvanize excite to action

gambit plot, strategy

gamut range, scope

gargantuan large

garner gather

garnish decorate

garrote stranglehold

garrulous talkative

gauche awkward

genealogy ancestry

generic general

genesis beginning

genetics study of heredity

genre kind, category

genteel elegant, refined

genuflect kneel in reverence

genuine authentic, sincere

geriatrics pertaining to old age

germane relevant

ghastly horrible

gibe heckle

gingivitis inflammation of the gums

gist essence (of an argument)

glabrous without hair

glaucoma disorder of the eye

glean gather

glib insincere manner

glower stare angrily

glut surplus, excess

glutton one who eats too much

gnarl deform

gnome dwarf-like being

goad encourage, provoke

googol a very large number

gorge stuff, satiate

gorgon ugly person

gormandize eat voraciously

gory bloody

gossamer thin and flimsy

Gothic medieval style of architecture

gouge overcharge

gracious kindness, politeness

gradient incline, rising by degrees

Quiz 14 (Antonyms)

Directions: Choose the word most opposite in meaning to the capitalized word. Answers are on page 100.

1. ASSIMILATE: (A) strive (B) adapt (C) synchronize (D) estrange (E) officiate

2. INADVERTENT: (A) accidental (B) disingenuous (C) forthright (D) inconsiderate (E) calculated

3. ABSCOND: (A) pilfer (B) replace (C) glean (D) substitute (E) surrender

4. FOMENT: (A) exhort (B) dissuade (C) cower (D) abet (E) fixate

5. EXTENUATE: (A) alleviate (B) preclude (C) worsen (D) subdue (E) justify

6. NONPAREIL: (A) consummate (B) juvenile (C) dutiful (D) ordinary (E) choice

7. REPUDIATE: (A) denounce (B) deceive (C) embrace (D) fib (E) generalize

8. NOXIOUS: (A) diffuse (B) latent (C) beneficial (D) unique (E) unjust

9. SUFFRAGE: (A) absence of charity (B) absence of franchise (C) absence of pain (D) absence of success (E) absence of malice

10. GLEAN: (A) gaffe (B) furor (C) gather (D) frolic (E) foist

gradual by degrees, changing slowly
grandiose impressive, large
granular grainy
grapple struggle
gratis free

gratitude thankfulness
gratuitous unwarranted, uncalled for
gratuity tip
gravamen the essential part of an accusation

gravity seriousness
gregarious sociable
grievous tragic, heinous
grimace expression of disgust
or pain
grisly gruesome
grovel crawl, obey, beg
grudging reluctant
guffaw laughter
guile deceit
gullible easily deceived
gusto great enjoyment
guttural throaty
gyrate whirl

H

habitat natural environment
habituate accustom
hackneyed trite
haggard gaunt
halcyon serene
hale healthy
hallucination delusion
hamper obstruct
hapless unlucky
harangue tirade
harass torment
harbinger forerunner
harbor give shelter, conceal
hardy healthy
harlequin clown
harp complain incessantly
harridan hag
harrowing distressing
harry harass

haughty arrogant
haven refuge
havoc destruction, chaos
hearsay gossip
hedonism the pursuit of
pleasure in life
heed follow advice
heedless careless
hegemony authority,
domination
hegira a journey to a more
pleasant place
heinous vile, atrocious
heliocentric having the sun as a
center
helix a spiral
helots slaves
herald harbinger
herbivorous feeding on plants
Herculean powerful, large
hermetic airtight, sealed
hermit one who lives in
solitude
herpetologist one who studies
reptiles
heterodox departing form
established doctrines
heuristic teaching device or
method
hew cut
heyday glory days, prime
hiatus interruption
hibernal wintry
hidalgo nobleman
hidebound prejudiced,
provincial

hideous horrible
hie to hasten
highbrow intellectual
hirsute bearded
histrionic overly dramatic
holograph written entirely by hand
homage respect
homely plain
homily sermon
homogeneous uniform
homonym words that are identical in spelling and pronunciation
hone sharpen
horde group
hortatory inspiring good deeds
hospice shelter
hovel shanty, cabin
hoyden tomboy
hubris arrogance
hue color
humane compassionate
humanities languages and literature
humility humbleness
hummock knoll, mound
humus soil
husbandry management
hybrid crossbreed
hydrophobia fear of water
hygienic sanitary

hymeneal pertaining to marriage
hymn religious song
hyperactive overactive
hyperbole exaggeration
hypertension elevated blood pressure
hypocritical deceiving, two-faced
hypoglycemic low blood sugar
hypothermia low body temperature

I

ibidem in the same place
ichthyology study of fish
iconoclast one who rails against sacred institutions
idiosyncrasy peculiarity
idyllic natural, picturesque
ignoble dishonorable
ilk class, clan
illicit unlawful
illimitable limitless
illusory fleeting, deceptive
illustrious famous
imbibe drink
imbue infuse
immaculate spotlessly clean
immaterial irrelevant
immense huge

Quiz 15 (Matching)

Match each word in the first column with its definition in the second column. Answers are on page 100.

1. GRANDIOSE	A.	drink
2. GRIEVOUS	B.	pertaining to marriage
3. HALCYON	C.	arrogance
4. HARLEQUIN	D.	prejudiced
5. HEDONISM	E.	teaching device or method
6. HEURISTIC	F.	the pursuit of pleasure in life
7. HIDEBOUND	G.	clown
8. HUBRIS	H.	serene
9. HYMENEAL	I.	heinous
10. IMBIBE	J.	impressive

immerse bathe, engross

imminent about to happen

immobile still

immolate sacrifice (especially by fire)

immunity exemption from prosecution

immure build a wall around

immutable unchangeable, absolute

impair injure

impale pierce

impartial not biased

impasse deadlock

impassioned fiery, emotional

impassive calm

impeach accuse, charge

impeccable faultless

impecunious indigent

impede hinder

impediment obstacle

impel urge, force

impending approaching, imminent

imperative vital, pressing

imperceptible slight, intangible

imperialism colonialism

imperil endanger

imperious domineering

impertinent insolent

imperturbable calm, unflappable

impervious impenetrable, unreceptive

impetuous impulsive

impetus stimulus, spark

impinge encroach, touch

implant instill

implausible unlikely, improbable

implement carry out, execute

implicate incriminate

implicit implied

implore entreat

45

implosion bursting inward

impolitic unwise, inappropriate

imponderable difficult to estimate

import meaning, significance

importune urgent request

imposing intimidating, stately

imposition intrusion, burden

impotent powerless

impound seize

imprecation curse, inculcate

impregnable invincible

impresario promoter

impressionable susceptible, easily influenced

impressionism a style of painting

imprimatur sanction

impromptu spontaneous

improvise invent

impudence insolence

impugn criticize, accuse

impulse inclination, sudden desire

impulsive to act suddenly

impunity exemption from harm

impute charge

in toto in full, entirely

inadvertent unintentional

inadvisable not recommended

inalienable that which cannot be taken away

inane vacuous, stupid

inanimate inorganic, lifeless

inaudible cannot be heard

inaugurate induct (with a ceremony)

inborn innate

incalculable immeasurable

incandescent brilliant

incantation chant

incapacitate disable

incarcerate imprison

incarnate embody, personify

incendiary inflammatory

incense enrage

incentive stimulus, inducement

incessant unceasing

incest sex among family members

inchoate just begun

incidental insignificant, minor

incinerate burn

incipient beginning

incision cut

incisive keen, penetrating

incite foment, provoke

incivility rudeness

inclement harsh, stormy

inclusive comprehensive

incognito disguised

incommunicado unable to communicate with others

incomparable peerless

incompatibility inability to live in harmony

Quiz 16 (Analogies)

Directions: Choose the pair that expresses a relationship most similar to that expressed in the capitalized pair. Answers are on page 100.

1. ANARCHY : GOVERNMENT ::

   (A) confederation : state
   (B) trepidation : courage
   (C) serenity : equanimity
   (D) surfeit : food
   (E) computer : hard drive

2. Galvanize : Charismatic Leader ::

   (A) jeer : fan
   (B) correct : charlatan
   (C) impeach : President
   (D) retreat : champion
   (E) moderate : arbiter

3. PARRY : BLOW ::

   (A) equivocate : question
   (B) cower : start
   (C) boomerang : backlash
   (D) cast : invective
   (E) browbeat : chastity

4. DISQUIETUDE : ANXIOUS ::

   (A) magnitude : unabridged
   (B) isolation : sequestered
   (C) cupidity : bellicose
   (D) embellishment : overstated
   (E) nonplus : perplexed

5. MILK : DRAIN ::

   (A) insult : commend
   (B) abstract : distend
   (C) extend : disregard
   (D) exploit : employ
   (E) assail : rescind

6. ABSTRUSE : CLEAR ::

   (A) nondescript : conspicuous
   (B) high-brow : indifferent
   (C) affable : agreeable
   (D) prominent : manifest
   (E) complex : hard

7. OMNISCIENT : KNOWLEDGE ::

   (A) saturnine : energy
   (B) complete : retraction
   (C) principled : method
   (D) inquisitive : science
   (E) boundless : expanse

8. STOKE : SMOTHER ::

   (A) incinerate : heat
   (B) animate : enervate
   (C) contest : decry
   (D) acknowledge : apprehend
   (E) garrote : asphyxiate

9. ORCHESTRA : MUSICIAN ::

   (A) story : comedian
   (B) band : singer
   (C) garden : leaf
   (D) troupe : actor
   (E) government : lawyer

10. MUTTER : INDISTINCT ::

   (A) define : easy
   (B) blunder : polished
   (C) articulate : well-spoken
   (D) expedite : completed
   (E) censure : histrionic

inconceivable unthinkable

incongruous out of place, absurd

inconsiderate thoughtless, insensitive

inconspicuous not noticeable

incontrovertible indisputable

incorporate combine

incorrigible unreformable

incredulous skeptical

increment step, increase

incriminate accuse

incubus nightmare

inculcate instill, indoctrinate

inculpate accuse

incumbent obligatory

incursion raid

indecent offensive, lewd

indecorous unseemly

indelible permanent

indemnity insurance

indict charge

indifferent unconcerned

indigenous native

indigent poor

indignant resentment of injustice

indiscreet lacking sound judgment, rash

indiscriminate random

indispensable vital, essential

indistinct blurry, without clear features

indolent lazy

indomitable invincible

indubitable unquestionable

induce persuade, provoke

indulge succumb to desire

indurate harden

industrious hard-working

inebriate intoxicate

ineffable inexpressible

ineffectual futile

ineluctable inescapable

inept unfit, incompetent

inert inactive

inestimable priceless, immeasurable

inevitable unavoidable, predestined

inexorable relentless

infallible unerring

infamous notorious

infamy shame

infantry foot soldiers

infatuate immature love

infer conclude

infernal hellish

infidel nonbeliever

infidelity disloyalty

infiltrate trespass

infinitesimal very small

infirmary clinic

infirmity ailment
inflammatory incendiary
influx inflow
infraction violation
infringe encroach
infuriate enrage
infuse inspire, instill
ingenious clever, resourceful
ingrate ungrateful person
ingratiate pleasing, flattering, endearing
ingress entering
inherent innate, inborn
inhibit restrain
inimical adverse, hostile
inimitable peerless
iniquitous unjust, wicked
iniquity sin, injustice
initiate begin
initiation induction ceremony
injunction command
inkling hint
innate inborn
innervate invigorate
innocuous harmless
innovative new, useful idea
innuendo insinuation
inopportune untimely
inordinate excessive
inquest investigation
inquisition interrogation
inquisitive curious
insatiable gluttonous
inscribe engrave

inscrutable cannot be fully understood
insensate without feeling
insidious treacherous, sinister
insignia emblems
insinuate allude
insipid flat, dull
insolent insulting
insolvent bankrupt
insouciant nonchalant
installment portion, payment
instant at once
instigate incite
insubordinate disobedient
insufferable unbearable
insular narrow-minded
insuperable insurmountable
insurgent rebellious
insurrection uprising
intangible not perceptible by touch
integral essential
integrate make whole
integration unification
integument a covering
intelligentsia the intellectual elite of society
intensive extreme, concentrated
inter bury
intercede plead on behalf of another
intercept prevent, cut off
interdict prohibit
interject interrupt

Quiz 17 (Matching)

Match each word in the first column with its definition in the second column. Answers are on page 100.

1.	INCONGRUOUS	A.	harden
2.	INCONSPICUOUS	B.	relentless
3.	INDECOROUS	C.	hostile
4.	INDIGNANT	D.	cannot be fully understood
5.	INDURATE	E.	out of place, absurd
6.	INEXORABLE	F.	not noticeable
7.	INIMICAL	G.	unseemly
8.	INSCRUTABLE	H.	resentment of injustice
9.	INSOUCIANT	I.	nonchalant
10.	INSUPERABLE	J.	insurmountable

---

interloper intruder

interlude intermission

interminable unending

internecine mutually destructive

interpolate insert

interpose insert

interregnum interval between two successive reigns

interrogate question

intersperse scatter

interstate between states

intervene interfere, mediate

intestate leaving no will

intimate allude to, hint

intractable unmanageable

intransigent unyielding

intrepid fearless

intricate complex

intrigue plot, mystery

intrinsic inherent

introspection self-analysis

inundate flood

inure accustom, habituate, harden

invalidate disprove, nullify

invective verbal insult

inveigh to rail against

inveigle lure, wheedle

inventive cleaver, resourceful

inverse directly opposite

inveterate habitual, chronic

invidious incurring ill-will

invincible cannot be defeated

inviolate sacred, unchangeable

invocation calling on God

irascible irritable

irate angry

ironic oddly contrary to what is expected

irrational illogical

irrelevant unrelated, immaterial

irreparable cannot be repaired

irresolute hesitant, uncertain

irrevocable cannot be rescinded
isosceles having two equal sides
itinerant wandering
itinerary route

juvenescent making young, growing out of infancy and into childhood
juxtapose to place side by side

J

jabberwocky nonsense
jaded spent, bored with one's situation
jargon specialized vocabulary
jaundiced biased, embittered
jeer mock
jejune barren, unsophisticated
jest joke
jilt reject, end a relationship promptly
jingoistic nationalistic, warmongering
jocular humorous
jostle push, brush against
journeyman reliable worker
joust combat between knights on horses
jubilant in high spirits
judicious prudent
juggernaut unstoppable force
jugular throat
juncture pivotal point in time
Junoesque stately beauty
junta small ruling group
jurisdiction domain
jurisprudence law
justify excuse, mitigate

K

kaleidoscope series of changing events
keen of sharp mind
ken purview, range of comprehension
kindle arouse, inspire
kindred similar, related by blood
kinetic pertaining to motion
kismet fate, the will of Allah
kite bad check
kitsch trashy art
kleptomania impulse to steal
knave con man
knead massage, to fold, press, and stretch a substance into a uniform mass
knell sound of a bell
Koran holy book of Islam
kowtow behave obsequiously
kudos acclaim

L

labyrinth maze
lacerate tear, cut

51

Quiz 18 (Analogies)

Directions: Choose the pair that expresses a relationship most similar to that expressed in the capitalized pair. Answers are on page 100.

1. Loquacious : Garrulous ::

    (A)   harsh : kindly
    (B)   animate : weary
    (C)   gluttonous : disloyal
    (D)   rash : impetuous
    (E)   blithe : gloomy

2. EMPATHY : FEELING ::

    (A)   melancholy : joy
    (B)   sibling : relative
    (C)   Spartan : wickedness
    (D)   boldness : guilt
    (E)   institution : encouragement

3. DEVIATE : LECTURE ::

    (A)   broadcast : information
    (B)   disown : friend
    (C)   welcome: indifference
    (D)   entreat : solicitation
    (E)   meander : drive

4. NEBULOUS : FORM ::

    (A)   insincere : misanthrope
    (B)   benevolent : excellence
    (C)   insipid : taste
    (D)   discerning : hope
    (E)   composed : innocence

5. PENSIVE : MELANCHOLY ::

    (A)   scornful : contempt
    (B)   confident : victory
    (C)   eloquent : optimism
    (D)   sorrowful : indifference
    (E)   contumacious : esteem

6. ANATHEMA : CURSE ::

    (A)   hex : blessing
    (B)   admonition : censure
    (C)   incantation : discernment
    (D)   theory : calculation
    (E)   conjecture : truth

7. DILIGENT : ASSIDUOUS ::

    (A)   suspicious : reliable
    (B)   cautious : indecisive
    (C)   repentant : innocent
    (D)   peerless : common
    (E)   indigent : poor

8. LAMPOON : MOCK::

    (A)   exalt : ennoble
    (B)   entice : disown
    (C)   prattle : talk
    (D)   entreat : controvert
    (E)   debate : heckle

9. INTUITIVE : CONSIDERED ::

    (A)   impromptu : planning
    (B)   laborious : safe
    (C)   ethereal : light
    (D)   random : sequential
    (E)   rational : certain

10. ETERNAL : EPHEMERAL ::

    (A)   equivocal : ambiguous
    (B)   hopeless : chance
    (C)   animated : blithe
    (D)   mysterious : perplexing
    (E)   foreign : familiar

lachrymose tearful

lackey servant

laconic brief, terse

lactic derived from milk

lacuna a missing part, gap

laggard loafer, slacker

lagniappe bonus

laity laymen

lambent softly radiant

lament mourn

lamina layer

lampoon satirize

languish weaken

lanyard short rope

larceny theft

largess generous donation

lascivious lustful

lassitude lethargy

latent potential, dormant

laudatory commendable

laurels fame, success

lave wash

lavish extravagant

lax loose, careless

laxity carelessness

layman nonprofessional

lectern reading desk

leery cautious, doubtful

legacy bequest

legerdemain trickery

legible readable

legislate make laws

legitimate lawful

lenient forgiving

lethargic drowsy, sluggish

levee embankment, dam

leviathan a monster

levity frivolity

liable legally responsible

liaison relationship, affair

libertarian one who believes in complete freedom

libertine roué, rake

libidinous lustful

licentious lewd, immoral

lien financial claim

lieutenant one who acts in place of another

ligature bond

ligneous wood like

Lilliputian very small

limerick poem

limn portray, describe

limpid transparent, clearly understood

linchpin something that is indispensable

lineage ancestry

linguistics study of language

liquidate eliminate

lissome agile, supple

listless lacking spirit or interest

litany list

lithe supple

litigate contest with a lawsuit

litotes two negative statement that cancel to make a positive statement

liturgy ceremony

livid enraged

loath reluctant

loathe abhor, dislike

lofty high

logistics means of supplying troops

logo symbol

logy sluggish

loquacious talkative

lothario rake, womanizer

lout goon, hoodlum

lucid clearly understood

lucrative profitable

lucre money, profit

ludicrous absurd

lugubrious extremely sad

luminous bright

lupine wolf-like

lure entice

lurid ghastly, sensational

luster gloss, sheen

luxuriant lush, lavish

lynch to execute by hanging without a trial

M

macabre gruesome

Machiavellian politically crafty, cunning

machination plot

macrobiosis longevity

macroscopic visibly large

maelstrom whirlpool

magisterial arbitrary, dictatorial

magnanimous generous, kindhearted

magnate a powerful, successful person (especially of business)

magnitude size

magnum opus masterpiece

maim injure, disfigure

maladjusted disturbed

maladroit clumsy

malady illness

malaise uneasiness, weariness

malapropism comical misuse of a word

malcontent one who is forever dissatisfied

malediction curse

malefactor evildoer

malevolence bad intent, malice

malfeasance wrong doing (especially by an official of government)

malice spite

malign defame

malignant virulent, pernicious

malinger shirk

malleable moldable, tractable

Quiz 19 (Matching)

Match each word in the first column with its definition in the second column. Answers are on page 100.

1.	LACHRYMOSE	A.	trickery
2.	LAGGARD	B.	roué
3.	LASCIVIOUS	C.	very small
4.	LEGERDEMAIN	D.	tearful
5.	LIBERTINE	E.	loafer
6.	LILLIPUTIAN	F.	lustful
7.	LOQUACIOUS	G.	talkative
8.	MACHIAVELLIAN	H.	comical misuse of a word
9.	MAGISTERIAL	I.	arbitrary, dictatorial
10.	MALAPROPISM	J.	politically crafty, cunning

malodorous fetid

mammoth huge

manacle shackle

mandate command

mandatory obligatory

mandrill baboon

mania madness, obsession

manifest obvious, evident

manifesto proclamation

manifold multiple, diverse

manslaughter killing another person without malice

manumit set free

manuscript unpublished book

mar damage

marauder plunderer

marginal insignificant

marionette puppet

maroon abandon

marshal array, mobilize

martial warlike

martinet disciplinarian

martyr sacrifice, symbol

masochist one who enjoys pain

masticate chew

mastiff large dog

mastodon extinct elephant

maternal motherly

maternity motherhood

matriarch matron

matriculate enroll (usually in school)

matrix array

matutinal early, morning

maudlin weepy, sentimental

maul rough up

mausoleum tomb

maverick a rebel, individualist

mawkish sickeningly sentimental

mayhem mutilation, chaos

mea culpa my fault

meager scanty

meander roam, ramble

55

median middle

mediocre average

medley mixture

megalith ancient stone monument

melancholy reflective, gloomy

melee riot

mellifluous sweet sounding

melodious melodic

memento souvenir

memoir autobiography

memorabilia things worth remembering

memorandum note

menagerie zoo

mendacity untruth

mendicant beggar

menial humble, degrading

mentor teacher

mercantile commercial

mercenary calculating, venal

mercurial changeable, volatile

metamorphosis a change in form

mete distribute

meteoric swift, dazzling

meteorology science of weather

methodical systematic, careful

meticulous extremely careful, precise

metier occupation

metonymy the substitution of a phrase for the name itself

mettle courage, capacity for bravery

miasma toxin fumes

mien appearance, bearing

migrate travel

milieu environment

militant combative, activist

militate work against

milk extract

millennium thousand-year period

minatory threatening

mince chop, moderate

minion subordinate

minstrel troubadour

minuscule small

minute very small

minutiae trivia

mirage illusion

mire marsh, a situation that is difficult to escape from

mirth jollity

misanthrope hater of mankind

misappropriation use dishonestly

misbegotten illegitimate, obtained by dishonest means

miscarry abort

miscegenation intermarriage between races

Quiz 20 (Analogies)

Directions: Choose the pair that expresses a relationship most similar to that expressed in the capitalized pair. Answers are on page 100.

1. SPEECH : FILIBUSTER ::

    (A) race : marathon
    (B) gift : breach
    (C) statement : digression
    (D) detour : path
    (E) address : postage

2. ARISTOCRAT : LAND ::

    (A) bureaucracy : enslavement
    (B) monarchy : abnegation
    (C) gentry : talent
    (D) dignitary : rank
    (E) junta : anarchy

3. SURREPTITIOUS : STEALTH ::

    (A) clandestine : openness
    (B) guarded : effrontery
    (C) bombastic : irreverence
    (D) pernicious : bane
    (E) impertinent : humility

4. PECCADILLO : FLAW ::

    (A) mediator : dispute
    (B) grammar : error
    (C) nick : score
    (D) forensics : judiciary
    (E) invasion : putsch

5. LEVEE : RIVER ::

    (A) rampart : barrier
    (B) cordon : throng
    (C) broker : investment
    (D) promontory : height
    (E) string : guitar

6. HEDONIST : UNSTINTING ::

    (A) protagonist : insignificant
    (B) thug : aggressive
    (C) politician : irresolute
    (D) benefactor : generous
    (E) drunkard : manifest

7. EXCERPT : NOVEL ::

    (A) critique : play
    (B) review : manuscript
    (C) swatch : cloth
    (D) foreword : preface
    (E) recital : performance

8. EXORCISM : DEMON ::

    (A) matriculation : induction
    (B) banishment : member
    (C) qualm : angel
    (D) heuristic : method
    (E) manifesto : spirit

9. HOPE : CYNICAL ::

    (A) reticence : benevolent
    (B) contention : bellicose
    (C) bliss : sullen
    (D) homage : industrious
    (E) unconcern : indifferent

10. Exhibitionist : Attention ::

    (A) sycophant : turmoil
    (B) scientist : power
    (C) megalomaniac : solitude
    (D) martyr : anonymity
    (E) mercenary : money

miscellany mixture of items

misconstrue misinterpret

miscreant evildoer

misgiving doubt, hesitation

misnomer wrongly named

misogyny hatred of women

misshapen deformed

missive letter

mitigate lessen the severity

mnemonics that which aids the memory

mobilize assemble for action

mobocracy rule by mob

modicum pittance

modish chic

module unit

mogul powerful person

molest bother, sexually assault

mollify appease

molten melted

momentous of great importance

monocle eyeglass

monolithic large and uniform

monologue long speech

monstrosity distorted, abnormal form

moot disputable, no longer relevant

moral ethical

morale spirit, confidence

morass swamp, difficult situation

moratorium postponement

mordant biting, sarcastic

mores moral standards

moribund near death

morose sullen

morphine painkilling drug

morsel bite, piece

mortify humiliate

mosque temple

mote speck

motif artistic theme

motive reason for doing something

motley diverse

mottled spotted

motto slogan, saying

mountebank charlatan

mousy drab, colorless

muckraker reformer

muffle stifle, quiet

mulct defraud

multifarious diverse, many-sided

multitude throng

mundane ordinary

munificent generous

murmur mutter, mumble

muse ponder

muster to gather one's forces

mutability able to change

mute silent

mutilate maim

mutiny rebellion
mutter murmur, grumble
muzzle restrain, stifle
myopic narrow-minded
myriad innumerable
myrmidons loyal followers
mystique mystery, aura
mythical fictitious

N

nadir lowest point
narcissism self-love
narrate tell, recount
nascent incipient
natal related to birth
nativity the process of birth
naturalize grant citizenship
ne'er-do-well loafer, idler
nebulous indistinct
necromancy sorcery
nefarious evil
negate cancel
negligible insignificant
nemesis implacable foe
neologism newly coined
expression
neonatal newborn
neophyte beginner
nepotism favoritism
nervy brash
nether under
nettle irritate
neurotic disturbed
neutralize offset, nullify

nexus a link between two or
more people or things
nicety euphemism
niche nook, an activity that well
suits a person's talents
niggardly stingy
nimble spry
nirvana bliss, the attainment of
spiritual enlightenment
noctambulism sleepwalking
nocturnal pertaining to night
nocturne serenade
noisome harmful, disgusting
nomad wanderer
nomenclature terminology
nominal slight, in name only
nominate propose, recommend
somebody for a position
nominee candidate
nonchalant casual
noncommittal neutral,
circumspect
nondescript lacking distinctive
features
nonentity person of no
significance
nonesuch paragon, one in a
thousand
nonpareil unequaled, peerless
nonpartisan neutral,
uncommitted
nonplus confound, befuddle
notable remarkable, noteworthy
noted famous
notorious wicked, widely
known
nouveau riche newly rich

Quiz 21 (Matching)

Match each word in the first column with its definition in the second column. Answers are on page 100.

1.	MISCELLANY	A.	peerless
2.	MISSIVE	B.	to gather one's forces
3.	MOOT	C.	newly coined expression
4.	MOUNTEBANK	D.	self-love
5.	MULTIFARIOUS	E.	loyal followers
6.	MUSTER	F.	letter
7.	MYRMIDONS	G.	diverse
8.	NARCISSISM	H.	charlatan
9.	NEOLOGISM	I.	disputable
10.	NONPAREIL	J.	mixture of items

---

nova bright star

novel new, unique

novice beginner

noxious toxic

nuance shade, subtlety

nub crux, crucial point

nubile marriageable

nugatory useless, worthless

nuisance annoyance

nullify void

nullity nothingness

numismatics coin collecting

nurture nourish, foster

nymph goddess

O

oaf awkward person

obdurate unyielding, hardhearted

obeisance homage, deference

obelisk tall column, monument

obese fat

obfuscate bewilder, muddle

obituary eulogy

objective (adj.) unbiased

objective (noun) goal

objectivity impartiality

oblation offering, sacrifice

obligatory required, compulsory

oblige compel

obliging accommodating, considerate

oblique indirect

obliquity perversity

obliterate destroy

oblong elliptical, oval

obloquy slander

obscure vague, unclear

obsequious fawning, servile

obsequy funeral ceremony

observant watchful

obsolete outdated

obstinate stubborn

obstreperous noisy, unruly

obtain gain possession

obtrusive forward, meddlesome

obtuse stupid

obviate make unnecessary

Occident the West

occlude block

occult mystical, secret, relating
to the supernatural or witchcraft

octogenarian person in her
eighties

ocular optic, visual

ode poem

odious despicable

odoriferous pleasant odor

odyssey journey

offal inedible parts of a
butchered animal

offertory church collection

officiate supervise

officious forward, obtrusive

offset counterbalance

ogle flirt

ogre monster, demon

oleaginous oily

oligarchy aristocracy

olio medley

ominous threatening

omnibus collection,
compilation

omnipotent all-powerful

omniscient all-knowing

onerous burdensome

onslaught powerful attack

ontology the study of the nature
of existence

onus burden

opaque nontransparent

operative working

operetta musical comedy

opiate narcotic

opine think, express an opinion

opportune well-timed,
appropriate

oppress persecute

oppressive burdensome

opprobrious abusive, scornful

opprobrium disgrace

oppugn assail

opt decide, choose

optimum best condition

optional elective

opulence wealth

opus literary work or musical
composition

oracle prophet

oration speech

orator speaker

orb sphere

orchestrate organize

ordain appoint

Quiz 22 (Analogies)

<u>Directions:</u> Choose the pair that expresses a relationship most similar to that expressed in the capitalized pair. Answers are on page 100.

1. PARAGRAPH : ESSAY ::

   (A) trailer : automobile
   (B) query : question
   (C) instrument : surgery
   (D) penmanship : essay
   (E) shot : salvo

2. COMPOUND : BUILDING ::

   (A) classroom : campus
   (B) department : government
   (C) tapestry : fabric
   (D) seed : vegetable
   (E) commonwealth : country

3. CONSTELLATION : STARS ::

   (A) amplifier : hearing
   (B) ocean : water
   (C) mosaic : tile
   (D) tracks : train
   (E) book : paper

4. ACCELERATE : VELOCITY ::

   (A) relinquish : assets
   (B) energize : stamina
   (C) protect : parent
   (D) project : futility
   (E) educate : stupor

5. SIDEREAL : STARS ::

   (A) platonic : radiation
   (B) avian : fish
   (C) corporeal : heaven
   (D) heliocentric : transportation
   (E) terrestrial : Earth

6. STATE : CONFEDERACY ::

   (A) apple : tree
   (B) return address : envelope
   (C) binoculars : sight
   (D) velocity : acceleration
   (E) soldier : army

7. HELPFUL : OFFICIOUS ::

   (A) difficult : incorrigible
   (B) maudlin : sardonic
   (C) apathetic : zealous
   (D) true : contrary
   (E) friendly : amiable

8. SATURATE : DAMPEN ::

   (A) contaminate : pollute
   (B) besmirch : sully
   (C) extol : praise
   (D) waive : donate
   (E) pronounce : presume

9. WAYLAY : ADVANCEMENT ::

   (A) corroborate : testimony
   (B) amuse : jeopardy
   (C) condescend : frenzy
   (D) curb : movement
   (E) negotiate : defeat

10. MITIGATE : INJURY ::

   (A) exacerbate : recovery
   (B) palliate : accusation
   (C) dampen : enthusiasm
   (D) darken : obscurity
   (E) entreat : ultimatum

orderly neat, arranged

ordinance law

ordnance artillery

orient align, familiarize

orison prayer

ornate lavishly decorated

ornithology study of birds

orthodox conventional

oscillate waver, swing

ossify harden

ostensible apparent, seeming

ostentatious pretentious

ostracize banish, shun

otherworldly spiritual

otiose idle

ouster ejection

outmoded out-of-date

outré eccentric

outset beginning

ovation applause

overrule disallow

overture advance, proposal

overweening arrogant, forward

overwhelm overpower

overwrought overworked, high-strung

ovum egg, cell

P

pachyderm elephant

pacifist one who opposes all violence

pacify appease

pact agreement

paean a song of praise

pagan heathen, ungodly

page attendant

pageant exhibition, show

pains great effort, attention to detail

painstaking taking great care, thorough

palatial grand, splendid

palaver babble, nonsense

Paleolithic stone age

paleontologist one who studies fossils

pall to become dull or weary

palliate assuage

pallid pale, sallow

palpable touchable

palpitate beat, throb

palsy paralysis

paltry scarce

pan criticize

panacea cure-all

panache flamboyance

pandemic widespread, plague

pandemonium din, commotion

pander cater to people's baser instincts

panegyric praise

pang short sharp pain

panoply full suit of armor

panorama vista

pant gasp, puff

pantomime mime

pantry storeroom

papyrus paper

parable allegory

paradigm a model

paragon standard of excellence

parameter limit

paramount chief, foremost

paramour lover

paranoid obsessively suspicious, demented

paranormal supernatural

parapet rampart, defense

paraphernalia equipment

paraphrase restatement

parcel package

parchment paper

pare peel

parenthetical in parentheses

pariah outcast

parish fold, church

parity equality

parlance local speech

parlay increase

parley conference

parochial provincial

parody imitation, ridicule

parole release

paroxysm outburst, convulsion

parrot mimic

parry avert, ward off

parsimonious stingy

parson clergyman

partake share, receive, consume

partial incomplete

partiality bias

parting farewell, severance

partisan supporter

partition division

parvenu newcomer, social climber

pasquinade satire

passé outmoded

passim here and there

pastel pale

pasteurize disinfect

pastoral rustic

patent obvious

paternal fatherly

pathetic pitiful

pathogen agent causing disease

pathogenic causing disease

pathos emotion

patrician aristocrat

patrimony inheritance

patronize condescend

patronymic a name formed form the name of a father

patter walk lightly

paucity scarcity

Quiz 23 (Matching)

Match each word in the first column with its definition in the second column. Answers are on page 100.

1.	ORDNANCE	A.	a model
2.	ORTHODOX	B.	local speech
3.	OUTMODED	C.	convulsion
4.	PALAVER	D.	stingy
5.	PANEGYRIC	E.	agent causing disease
6.	PARADIGM	F.	artillery
7.	PARLANCE	G.	conventional
8.	PAROXYSM	H.	out-of-date
9.	PARSIMONIOUS	I.	babble
10.	PATHOGEN	J.	praise

paunch stomach

pauper poor person

pavilion tent

pawn (noun) tool, stooge

pawn (verb) pledge

pax peace

peaked wan, pale, haggard

peal reverberation, outburst

peccadillo a minor fault

peculate embezzle

peculiar unusual

peculiarity characteristic

pedagogical pertaining to teaching

pedagogue dull, formal teacher

pedant pedagogue

pedantic bookish

peddle sell

pedestrian common

pedigree genealogy

peerage aristocracy

peevish cranky

pejorative insulting

pell-mell in a confused manner

pellucid transparent

pen write

penance atonement

penchant inclination

pend depend, hang

pending not decided, awaiting

penitent repentant

pensive sad

penurious stingy

penury poverty

peon common worker

per se in itself

perceptive discerning

percolate ooze, permeate

perdition damnation

peregrination wandering

peremptory dictatorial

perennial enduring, lasting

perfectionist purist, precisionist

65

perfidious treacherous (of a person)
perforate puncture
perforce by necessity
perfunctory careless
perigee point nearest to the earth
perilous dangerous
peripatetic walking about
periphery outer boundary
perish die
perishable decomposable
perjury lying
permeate spread throughout
permutation reordering
pernicious destructive, evil
peroration conclusion
perpendicular at right angles
perpetrate commit
perpetual continuous, everlasting
perpetuate cause to continue
perpetuity eternity
perplex puzzle, bewilder
perquisite reward, bonus
persecute harass
persevere persist, endure
persona social facade
personable charming, friendly
personage official, dignitary
personify embody, exemplify
personnel employees

perspicacious keen
perspicacity discernment, keenness
persuasive convincing
pert flippant, bold
pertain to relate
pertinacious persevering
pertinent relevant
perturbation agitation
peruse read carefully
pervade permeate
pessimist cynic, naysayer
pestilence disease
petite small
petition a written request
petrify calcify, shock
petrology study of rocks
pettifogger unscrupulous lawyer
petty trivial, niggling
petulant irritable, peevish
phantasm apparition
phenomena unusual natural events
philanthropic charitable
philanthropist altruist
philatelist stamp collector
philippic invective
Philistine barbarian
philosophical contemplative

Quiz 24 (Analogies)

Directions: Choose the pair that expresses a relationship most similar to that expressed in the capitalized pair. Answers are on page 100.

1. SECLUSION : HERMIT ::

    (A) wealth: embezzler
    (B) ambition : philanthropist
    (C) domination : athlete
    (D) turpitude : introvert
    (E) injustice : lawyer

2. ASCETIC : SELF-DENIAL ::

    (A) soldier : safety
    (B) official : charity
    (C) thug : acceptance
    (D) benefactor : competition
    (E) profligate : squandering

3. Philanthropist : Altruism ::

    (A) authoritarian : indulgence
    (B) polemicist : Marxist
    (C) benefactor : heir
    (D) pragmatist : hard-liner
    (E) libertarian : liberty

4. RACONTEUR : ANECDOTE ::

    (A) cynosure : interest
    (B) politician : corruption
    (C) athlete : perfection
    (D) writer : publication
    (E) nonentity : fame

5. PATENT : MANIFEST ::

    (A) credulous : gullible
    (B) truculent : nonchalant
    (C) lissome : spiritless
    (D) covert : prolific
    (E) cloyed : insufficient

6. Censorious : Condoning ::

    (A) inattentive : neglectful
    (B) cursory : inept
    (C) defunct : exquisite
    (D) perfunctory : thorough
    (E) munificent : generous

7. PURGE : OPPONENT ::

    (A) entrench : comrade
    (B) elevate : criminal
    (C) liquidate : politician
    (D) desalinize : salt
    (E) assuage : reactionary

8. ISLAND : ATOLL ::

    (A) peninsula : archipelago
    (B) fire : spring
    (C) hand : glove
    (D) utensil : fork
    (E) smock : instrument

9. MNEMONIC : MEMORY ::

    (A) demonstration : manifestation
    (B) pacemaker : heartbeat
    (C) sanction : recall
    (D) rhetoric : treatise
    (E) impasse : fruition

10. EAT : GORGE ::

    (A) sprint : jog
    (B) snicker : smirk
    (C) read : write
    (D) disengage : attack
    (E) drink : guzzle

phlegmatic sluggish

phobia fear

phoenix rebirth

physic laxative, cathartic

physique frame, musculature

picaresque roguish, adventurous

picayune trifling

piecemeal one at a time

pied mottled, brindled

piety devoutness

pilfer steal

pillage plunder

pillory punish by ridicule

pine languish, to long for someone or something

pinnacle highest point

pious devout, holy

piquant tart-tasting, spicy

pique sting, arouse interest

piscine pertaining to fish

piteous sorrowful, pathetic

pithy concise

pitiable miserable, wretched

pittance alms, driblet

pittance trifle

pivotal crucial

pixilated eccentric, possessed

placard poster

placate appease

placid serene

plagiarize pirate, counterfeit

plaintive expressing sorrow

platitude trite remark

platonic nonsexual

plaudit acclaim

pleasantry banter, persiflage

plebeian common, vulgar

plebiscite referendum

plenary full

plentiful abundant

pleonasm redundancy, verbosity

plethora overabundance

pliable flexible

pliant supple, flexible

plight sad situation

plucky courageous

plumb measure

plummet sudden shortfall

plutocrat wealthy person

plutonium radioactive material

poach steal

podgy fat

podium stand, rostrum

pogrom massacre, mass murder

poignant pungent, sharp, heartbreaking

polemic a controversy

polity methods of government

poltroon dastard

polychromatic many-colored

polygamist one who has many wives

ponder muse, reflect

ponderous heavy, bulky

pontiff bishop

pontificate to speak at length

poltroon coward

porcine pig-like

porous permeable, spongy

porridge stew

portend signify, augur

portent omen

portly large

portmanteau suitcase

posit stipulate

posterior rear, subsequent

posterity future generations

posthaste hastily

posthumous after death

postulate supposition, premise

potent powerful

potentate sovereign, king

potion brew

potpourri medley

potter aimlessly busy

pragmatic practical

prate babble

prattle chatter

preamble introduction

precarious dangerous, risky

precedent an act that serves as an example

precept principle, law

precinct neighborhood

precipice cliff

precipitate cause

precipitous steep

précis summary

precise accurate, detailed

preclude prevent

precocious more developed than is expected at a particular age

preconception prejudgment, prejudice

precursor forerunner

predacious plundering

predecessor one who proceeds

predestine foreordain

predicament quandary

predicate to base an opinion on something

predilection inclination

predisposed inclined

preeminent supreme

preempt commandeer

preen groom

prefabricated ready-built

prefect magistrate

preference choice

preferment promotion

prelate primate, bishop

preliminary introductory

prelude introduction

premeditate plan in advance

premonition warning

prenatal before birth

Quiz 25 (Matching)

Match each word in the first column with its definition in the second column. Answers are on page 101.

1.	PHOENIX	A.	cliff
2.	PILLORY	B.	inclination
3.	PITTANCE	C.	warning
4.	PLAUDIT	D.	acclaim
5.	PLETHORA	E.	overabundance
6.	POGROM	F.	after death
7.	POSTHUMOUS	G.	massacre
8.	PRECIPICE	H.	rebirth
9.	PREDILECTION	I.	punish by ridicule
10.	PREMONITION	J.	trifle

preponderance predominance

prepossessing appealing, charming

preposterous ridiculous

prerequisite requirement

prerogative right, privilege

presage omen

prescribe urge

presentable acceptable, well-mannered

preside direct, chair

pressing urgent

prestidigitator magician

prestige reputation, renown

presume assume, deduce

presumptuous assuming, overconfident

presuppose assume

pretense affectation, excuse

pretentious affected, inflated

preternatural abnormal, supernatural

pretext excuse

prevail triumph

prevailing common, current

prevalent widespread

prevaricate lie

prick puncture

priggish pedantic, affected

prim formal, prudish

primal first, beginning

primate head, master

primogeniture first-born child

primp groom

princely regal, generous

prismatic many-colored, sparkling

pristine pure, unspoiled

privation hardship

privy aware of private matters

probe examine

probity integrity

problematic uncertain, difficult

proboscis snout

procedure method, process

proceeds profit

proclaim announce

proclivity inclination

procreate beget

proctor supervise

procure acquire

procurer pander

prod urge

prodigal wasteful

prodigious marvelous, enormous

prodigy a person with extraordinary ability or talent

profane blasphemous

profess affirm, admit

proffer bring forward for consideration

proficient skillful

profiteer extortionist

profligate licentious, prodigal

profound deep, knowledgeable

profusion overabundance

progenitor ancestor

progeny children

prognosis forecast

prognosticate foretell

progressive advancing, liberal

proletariat working class

proliferate increase rapidly

prolific fruitful, productive

prolix long-winded

prologue introduction

prolong lengthen in time

promenade stroll, parade

promethean inspirational

promiscuous sexually indiscreet

promontory headland, cape

prompt induce

prompter reminder

promulgate publish, disseminate

prone inclined, predisposed

propaganda publicity, misinformation

propellant rocket fuel

propensity inclination

prophet prognosticator

prophylactic preventive

propinquity nearness

propitiate satisfy

propitious auspicious, favorable

proponent supporter, advocate

proportionate commensurate

proposition offer, proposal

propound propose

proprietor manager, owner

propriety decorum

prosaic uninspired, flat

proscenium platform, rostrum

proscribe prohibit

proselytize recruit, convert

prosody study of poetic structure

Quiz 26 (Analogies)

<u>Directions:</u> Choose the pair that expresses a relationship most similar to that expressed in the capitalized pair. Answers are on page 101.

1. CALLOUS : SYMPATHY ::

    (A)   flawless : excellence
    (B)   histrionic : theatrics
    (C)   outgoing : inhibition
    (D)   indiscreet : platitude
    (E)   categorical : truism

2. INSIPID : TASTE ::

    (A) curt : incivility
    (B) apathetic : zest
    (C) immaculate : brevity
    (D) trite : unimportance
    (E) discriminating : scholarship

3. Apocryphal : Corroboration ::

    (A)   didactic : instruction
    (B)   fraudulent : forgery
    (C)   tyrannical : poise
    (D)   esoteric : commonality
    (E)   sacrilegious : piety

4. NEBULOUS : DISTINCTION ::

    (A)   guileless : deceit
    (B)   antipathetic : abhorrence
    (C)   sublime : disrespect
    (D)   magnanimous : anxiety
    (E)   amorphous : inchoation

5. TARNISH : VITIATE ::

    (A)   beleaguer : console
    (B)   abrogate : flicker
    (C)   ensconce : corrupt
    (D)   bemuse : stupefy
    (E)   inundate : squelch

6. NOCTURNAL : CIMMERIAN ::

    (A)   exacting : lax
    (B)   prudish : indulgent
    (C)   contentious : affluent
    (D)   stark : embellished
    (E)   specious : illusory

7. CONVOCATION : MEETING ::

    (A)   bargain : market
    (B)   supplication : prayer
    (C)   issue : referendum
    (D)   speech : podium
    (E)   harvest : fall

8. OSTRICH : BIRD ::

    (A)   dusk : day
    (B)   fish : ocean
    (C)   tunnel : mountain
    (D)   hat : coat
    (E)   sirocco : storm

9. VIRUS : ORGANISM ::

    (A)   vegetable : mineral
    (B)   test-tube : bacteria
    (C)   microcosm : world
    (D)   microfiche : computer
    (E)   watch : wrist

10. Mercurial : Temperament ::

    (A)   capricious : interest
    (B)   tempestuous : solemnity
    (C)   staid : wantonness
    (D)   phlegmatic : concern
    (E)   cynical : naiveté

prospective expected, imminent

prospectus brochure

prostrate supine

protagonist main character in a story

protean changing readily

protégé ward, pupil

protocol code of diplomatic etiquette

proton particle

protract prolong

protuberance bulge

provender food

proverb maxim

proverbial well-known

providence foresight, divine protection

provident having foresight, thrifty

providential fortunate

province bailiwick, district

provincial intolerant, insular

provisional temporary

proviso stipulation

provisory conditional

provocation incitement

provocative titillating

provoke incite

prowess strength, expertise

proximity nearness

proxy substitute, agent

prude puritan

prudence discretion, carefulness

prudent cautious, using good judgment

prudish puritanical

prurient lewd

pseudo false

pseudonym alias

psychic pertaining the psyche or mind

psychopath madman

psychotic demented

puberty adolescence

puckish impish, mischievous

puerile childish

pugilism boxing

pugnacious combative

puissant strong

pulchritude beauty

pulp paste, mush

pulpit platform, priesthood

pulsate throb

pulverize crush

pun wordplay

punctilious meticulous

pundit learned or politically astute person

pungent sharp smell or taste

punitive punishing

puny weak, small

purblind obtuse, stupid

purgative cathartic, cleansing

purgatory limbo, netherworld

purge cleanse, remove

puritanical prim

purlieus environs, surroundings

purloin steal

purport claim to be

purported rumored

purposeful determined

pursuant following, according

purvey deliver, provide

purview range of understanding, field

pusillanimous cowardly

putative reputed

putrefy decay

putsch a sudden attempt to overthrow a government

pygmy dwarf

pyrotechnics fireworks

pyrrhic a battle won with unacceptable losses

Q

quack charlatan

quadrennial occurring every four years

quadrille square dance

quadruped four foot animal

quaff drink

quagmire difficult situation

quail shrink, cower

quaint old-fashioned, charming

qualified limited

qualms misgivings

quandary dilemma

quantum quantity, particle

quarantine detention, confinement

quarry prey, game

quarter residence, district

quash put down, suppress

quasi seeming, almost

quaver tremble

quay wharf

queasy squeamish

queer odd

quell suppress, allay

quench extinguish, slake

querulous complaining

questionnaire survey, feedback

queue line

quibble bicker

quicken revive, hasten

quiddity essence, an unimportant or trifling distinction

quiescent still, motionless

quietus a cessation of activity

quill feather, pen

quip joke

quirk eccentricity, a strange and unexpected turn of events

quiver tremble

quixotic impractical, romantic

quizzical odd, questioning

quorum the minimum number people who must be present to hold a meeting

quota a share or proportion

quotidian daily

Quiz 27 (Matching)

Match each word in the first column with its definition in the second column. Answers are on page 101.

1.	PROTEAN	A.	bulge
2.	PROTUBERANCE	B.	changing readily
3.	PROVISIONAL	C.	steal
4.	PUNDIT	D.	majority
5.	PURLOIN	E.	temporary
6.	PURPORT	F.	a cessation of activity
7.	QUAVER	G.	line
8.	QUEUE	H.	tremble
9.	QUIETUS	I.	claim to be
10.	QUORUM	J.	politically astute person

R

rabble crowd

rabid mad, furious

racketeer gangster, swindler

raconteur storyteller

radical revolutionary

raffish rowdy, dashing

rail rant, harangue

raiment clothing

rake womanizer

rally assemble

rambunctious boisterous

ramification consequence

rampage run amuck

rampant unbridled, raging

ramrod rod

rancid rotten

rancor resentment

randy vulgar

rankle cause bitterness, resentment

rant rage, scold

rapacious grasping, avaricious

rapidity speed

rapier sword

rapine plunder

rapport affinity, empathy

rapprochement reconciliation

rapture bliss

rash hasty, brash

rasp scrape

ratify approve

ration allowance, portion

rationale justification

ravage plunder, ruin

ravish captivate, charm

raze destroy or level a building

realm kingdom, domain

realpolitik cynical interpretation of politics

reap harvest

rebuff reject, snub

rebuke criticize, reprimand

rebus picture puzzle

rebuttal reply, counterargument

recalcitrant stubbornly resisting the authority of another

recant retract a previous statement

recapitulate restate, summarize

recede move back

receptacle container

receptive open to ideas

recidivism habitual criminal activity

recipient one who receives

reciprocal mutual, return in kind

recital performance, concert

recitation recital, lesson

reclusive solitary

recoil flinch, retreat

recollect remember

recompense repay, compensate

reconcile adjust, balance

recondite mystical, profound

reconnaissance surveillance

reconnoiter to survey, to scout (especially for military purposes)

recount recite

recoup recover

recourse appeal, resort

recreant cowardly

recrimination countercharge, retaliation

recruit draftee

rectify correct, to make right

recumbent reclining

recuperation recovery

recur repeat, revert

redeem buy back, justify, restore yourself to favor or to good opinion

redeemer savior

redemption salvation

redolent fragrant

redoubt fort

redoubtable formidable, steadfast

redress restitution, compensation

redundant repetitious

reek smell

reel stagger, to lurch backward as though struck by a blow

referendum vote

refined purified, cultured

reflux ebb

refraction bending, deflection

refractory obstinate, disobedient

refrain abstain

refurbish remodel, renovate

refute disprove, contradict

regal royal

regale entertain

regalia emblems

Quiz 28 (Analogies)

Directions: Choose the pair that expresses a relationship most similar to that expressed in the capitalized pair. Answers are on page 101.

1. PLUMMET : FALL ::

   (A) rifle : search
   (B) accelerate : stop
   (C) interdict : proscribe
   (D) rake : scour
   (E) precipitate : ascend

2. DRONE : EMOTION ::

   (A) sprint : journey
   (B) annoy : emollient
   (C) stupefy : erudition
   (D) deadpan : expression
   (E) scuttle : ship

3. MAROON : SEQUESTER ::

   (A) transfix : emote
   (B) exhaust : innervate
   (C) tranquilize : qualify
   (D) select : rebuff
   (E) entreat : beseech

4. TOTTER : WALK ::

   (A) annex : land
   (B) fathom : enlightenment
   (C) distend : contusion
   (D) efface : consolation
   (E) stutter : speech

5. LIGHT : DIM ::

   (A) indictment : investigate
   (B) protest : muffle
   (C) heat : radiate
   (D) solid : incinerate
   (E) ornament : decorate

6. BENIGN : PERNICIOUS ::

   (A) ostentatious : tawdry
   (B) mortified : nefarious
   (C) apocryphal : categorical
   (D) discerning : keen
   (E) pejorative : vicarious

7. Demagogue : Manipulator ::

   (A) champion : defender
   (B) lawyer : mediator
   (C) mentor : oppressor
   (D) soldier : landowner
   (E) capitalist : socialist

8. Gregarious : Congenial ::

   (A) suspicious : trusting
   (B) pedantic : lively
   (C) bellicose : militant
   (D) singular : nondescript
   (E) seminal : apocalyptic

9. DISHEARTENED : HOPE ::

   (A) enervated : ennui
   (B) buoyant : effervescence
   (C) amoral : ethics
   (D) munificent : altruism
   (E) nefarious : turpitude

10. PRATTLE : SPEAK ::

   (A) accept : reject
   (B) stomp : patter
   (C) heed : listen
   (D) promenade : walk
   (E) ejaculate : shout

regime a government

regiment infantry unit

regrettable lamentable, unfortunate

regurgitate vomit, repeat

rehash wearily discuss again

reign rule, influence

rein curb, restrain

reincarnation rebirth

reiterate repeat, say again

rejoice celebrate

rejoinder answer, retort

rejuvenate make young again

relapse recurrence (of illness)

relegate assign to an inferior position

relent soften, yield

relentless unstoppable

relic antique

relinquish release, renounce

relish savor

remedial corrective

remiss negligent

remit forgive, send payment

remnant residue, fragment

remonstrance protest

remorse guilt

remuneration compensation

renaissance rebirth

renascent reborn

rend to tear apart

render deliver, provide

rendezvous a meeting

rendition version, interpretation

renege break a promise

renounce disown

renown fame

rent tear, rupture

reparation amends, atonement

repartee witty conversation

repatriate to send back to the native land

repellent causing aversion

repent atone for

repercussion consequence

repertoire stock of works

repine fret

replenish refill

replete complete

replica copy

replicate duplicate

repose rest

reprehensible blameworthy

repress suppress

reprieve temporary suspension

reprimand rebuke

reprisal retaliation

reprise repetition

reproach blame

reprobate miscreant

reprove rebuke

repudiate disavow

repugnant distasteful, revolting

repulse repel

repulsive repugnant

repute status, reputation, esteem

reputed supposed, presumed, alleged

requiem rest, a mass for the dead

requisite necessary

requisition order, formal demand

requite to return in kind

rescind revoke

reserve self-control

reside dwell

residue remaining part

resigned accepting of a situation

resilience ability to recover from an illness or a setback

resolute determined

resolution determination

resolve determination

resonant reverberating

resort recourse

resound echo

resourceful inventive, skillful

respectively in that order

respire breathe

respite rest, temporary delay

resplendent shining, splendid

restitution reparation, amends

restive nervous, uneasy

resurgence revival

resurrection rebirth

resuscitate revive

retain keep

retainer advance fee

retaliate revenge

retch vomit

reticent reserved

retiring modest, unassuming

retort quick reply

retrench cut back, economize

retribution reprisal

retrieve reclaim

retrograde regress

retrospective reminiscent, display

revamp recast

reveille bugle call

revel frolic, take joy in

revelry merrymaking

revenue income

revere honor

reverent respectful

reverie daydream

revert return to a former state

revile denounce, defame

revision new version

revive renew

revoke repeal

revulsion aversion

rhapsody ecstasy

rhetoric elocution, grandiloquence

rheumatism inflammation

ribald coarse, vulgar

Quiz 29 (Matching)

Match each word in the first column with its definition in the second column. Answers are on page 101.

1.	REGIME	A.	vulgar
2.	REJOINDER	B.	quick reply
3.	REMUNERATION	C.	uneasy
4.	RENDEZVOUS	D.	necessary
5.	RENT	E.	miscreant
6.	REPROBATE	F.	rupture
7.	REQUISITE	G.	a meeting
8.	RESTIVE	H.	compensation
9.	RETRIBUTION	I.	retort
10.	RIBALD	J.	a government

---

rickety shaky, ramshackle

ricochet carom, rebound

rife widespread, abundant

riffraff dregs of society

rifle search through and steal

rift a split, an opening, disagreement

righteous upright, moral

rigor harshness, precise and exacting

rime crust

riposte counterthrust

risible laughable

risqué off-color, racy

rivet engross

robust vigorous

rogue scoundrel

roister bluster

romp frolic

roseate rosy, optimistic

roster list of people

rostrum podium

roué libertine

rouse awaken, provoke

rout vanquish, cause to retreat

rubicund ruddy complexion

ruck the common herd

rudiment beginning, kernel

rue regret

ruffian brutal person

ruminate ponder

rummage hunt, grope

runnel stream

ruse trick

rustic rural

S

Sabbath day of rest

sabbatical vacation

saber sword

sabotage treason, destruction

saccharine sugary, overly sweet tone

80

sacerdotal priestly

sack pillage

sacrament rite

sacred cow idol, taboo

sacrilege blasphemy

sacrosanct sacred

saddle encumber

sadist one who takes pleasure in hurting others

safari expedition

saga story

sagacious wise

sage wise person

salacious licentious

salient prominent

saline salty

sallow sickly complected

sally sortie, attack

salutary good, wholesome

salutation salute, greeting

salvation redemption

salve medicinal ointment

salvo volley, gunfire

sanctify consecrate

sanctimonious self-righteous

sanction approval

sanctuary refuge

sang-froid coolness under fire

sanguinary gory, murderous

sanguine cheerful

sans without

sapid interesting

sapient wise

sarcophagus stone coffin

scornful contemptuous

sartorial pertaining to clothes

satanic pertaining to the Devil

satchel bag

sate satisfy fully

satiate satisfy fully

satire ridicule

saturate soak

saturnine gloomy

satyr demigod, goat-man

saunter stroll

savanna grassland

savant scholar

savoir-faire tact, polish

savor enjoy, relish

savory appetizing

savvy perceptive, shrewd

scabrous difficult

scant inadequate, meager

scapegoat one who takes blame for others

scarify criticize

scathe injure, denounce

Quiz 30 (Analogies)

Directions: Choose the pair that expresses a relationship most similar to that expressed in the capitalized pair. Answers are on page 101.

1. THIMBLE : FINGER ::

    (A) glove : hammer
    (B) stitch : loop
    (C) branch : flower
    (D) talon : eagle
    (E) smock : apparel

2. ANARCHY : ORDER ::

    (A) desolation : annihilation
    (B) ineptitude : skill
    (C) bastion : aegis
    (D) chaos : disarray
    (E) parsimony : elegance

3. LAND : FALLOW ::

    (A) automobile : expensive
    (B) politics : innovative
    (C) orchard : fruitful
    (D) mountain : precipitous
    (E) ship : decommissioned

4. HEURISTIC : TEACH ::

    (A) parable : obfuscate
    (B) performer : entertain
    (C) pedant : construct
    (D) actor : incite
    (E) virus : prevent

5. RUSE : DECEIVE ::

    (A) pretext : mollify
    (B) invective : laud
    (C) cathartic : cleanse
    (D) artifice : disabuse
    (E) calumny : confuse

6. RETICENT : WANTON ::

    (A) lithe : supple
    (B) exemplary : palpable
    (C) pejorative : opprobrious
    (D) quiescent : rampant
    (E) provincial : virulent

7. GULLIBLE : DUPE ::

    (A) artless : demagogue
    (B) Machiavellian : entrepreneur
    (C) cantankerous : curmudgeon
    (D) disputatious : patron
    (E) optimistic : defeatist

8. OPAQUE : LIGHT ::

    (A) porous : liquid
    (B) undamped : vibration
    (C) unrelenting : barbarian
    (D) diaphanous : metal
    (E) hermetic : air

9. QUIXOTIC : PRAGMATIC ::

    (A) romantic : fanciful
    (B) dispassionate : just
    (C) auspicious : sanguine
    (D) malcontent : jingoistic
    (E) optimistic : surreal

10. COLON : INTRODUCE ::

    (A) hyphen : join
    (B) semicolon : transfer
    (C) dash : shorten
    (D) apostrophe : intensify
    (E) comma : possess

scepter a rod, staff

scheme plot, system, diagram

schism rift

scintilla speck

scintillate sparkle

scion offspring

scoff jeer, dismiss

scone biscuit

scorn disdain, reject

scoundrel unprincipled person

scour clean by rubbing, search

scourge affliction

scruples misgivings

scrupulous principled, fastidious

scrutinize examine closely

scurf dandruff

scurrilous abusive, insulting

scurry move quickly

scuttle to sink (a ship)

scythe long, curved blade

sear burn

sebaceous like fat

secede withdraw

secluded remote, isolated

seclusion solitude

sectarian denominational

secular worldly, nonreligious

secure make safe

sedation state of calm

sedentary stationary, inactive

sedition treason, inciting rebellion

seduce lure

sedulous diligent

seedy rundown, ramshackle

seemly proper, attractive

seethe fume, resent

seismic pertaining to earthquakes

seismology study of earthquakes

self-effacing modest

semantics study of word meanings

semblance likeness

seminal fundamental, decisive

semper fidelis always loyal

senescence old age

senescent aging

seniority privilege due to length of service

sensational outstanding, startling

sensible wise, prudent

sensory relating to the senses

sensualist epicure

sensuous appealing to the senses, enjoying luxury

sententious concise

sentient conscious

sentinel watchman

sepulcher tomb

sequacious dependent

sequel continuation, epilogue

sequester segregate

seraphic angelic

serendipity a knack for making fortunate discoveries

serene peaceful

serpentine winding and twisting

serried saw-toothed

serum vaccine

servile slavish

servitude forced labor

sessile permanently attached

session meeting

settee seat, sofa

sever cut in two

severance division

shallot onion

sham pretense, imposter

shambles disorder, mess

shard sharp fragment of glass

sheen luster

sheepish shy, embarrassed

shibboleth password

shirk evade (work)

sliver fragment, shaving

shoal reef

shoring supporting

shortcomings personal deficiencies

shrew virago

shrewd clever, cunning

shrill high-pitched

shun avoid, spurn

shunt turn aside

shyster unethical lawyer

sibilant a hissing sound

sibling brother or sister

sickle semicircular blade

sidereal pertaining to the stars

sidle move sideways, slither

siege blockade

sierra mountain range

sieve strainer

signatory signer

signet a seal

silhouette outline, profile

silo storage tower

simian monkey

simile figure of speech

simper smile, smirk

simulacrum vague likeness

sinecure position with little responsibility

sinewy fibrous, stringy

singe burn just the surface of something

singly one by one, individually

singular unique, extraordinary

sinister evil, malicious

sinistral left-handed

siphon extract, tap

sire forefather, to beget

siren temptress

site location

skeptical doubtful

skinflint miser

skirmish a small battle

Quiz 31 (Matching)

Match each word in the first column with its definition in the second column. Answers are on page 101.

1.	SCRUPLES	A.	figure of speech
2.	SCYTHE	B.	proper, attractive
3.	SEEMLY	C.	long, curved blade
4.	SENTENTIOUS	D.	left-handed
5.	SERENDIPITY	E.	pertaining to the stars
6.	SHIBBOLETH	F.	signer
7.	SIDEREAL	G.	making fortunate discoveries
8.	SIGNATORY	H.	password
9.	SIMILE	I.	misgivings
10.	SINISTRAL	J.	concise

skittish excitable, wary, jumpy

skulk sneak about

skullduggery trickery

slake quench

slander defame

slate list of candidate

slaver drivel, fawn

slay kill

sleight dexterity, skill

slew an abundance

slither slide, slink

slogan motto

sloth laziness

slovenly sloppy

smattering superficial knowledge

smelt refine metal

smirk smug look

smite strike, afflict

smock apron

snare trap

snide sarcastic, spiteful

snippet morsel, small piece

snivel whine, sniff

snub ignore, slight

snuff extinguish

sobriety composed, abstinent, sober

sobriquet nickname

socialite one who is prominent in society

sociology study of society

sodality companionship

sodden soaked

sojourn trip, stopover

solace consolation, comfort

solder fuse, weld

solecism ungrammatical construction

solemn serious, somber

solemnity seriousness

solicit request

solicitous considerate, concerned

85

soliloquy monologue

solstice furthest point

soluble dissolvable

solvent financially sound

somatic pertaining to the body

somber gloomy, solemn

somnambulist sleepwalker

somnolent sleepy

sonnet short poem

sonorous resonant, majestic

sop morsel, compensation, offering

sophistry specious reasoning

soporific sleep inducing

soprano high female voice

sordid foul, ignoble

sorority sisterhood

soubrette actress, ingenue

souse a drunk

sovereign monarch

spar fight

spasmodic intermittent, fitful

spate sudden outpouring

spawn produce

specimen sample

specious false but plausible reasoning

spectacle public display

spectral ghostly

spectrum range, gamut

speculate conjecture

speleologist one who studies caves

spew eject

spindle shaft

spindly tall and thin

spinster old maid

spire pinnacle

spirited lively

spirituous alcohol, intoxicating

spite malice, grudge

spittle spit

splay spread apart

spleen resentment, wrath

splenetic peevish

splurge indulge

spontaneous extemporaneous

sporadic occurring irregularly

sportive playful

spry nimble

spume foam, froth

spurious false, counterfeit

spurn to reject a person with scorn

squalid filthy

squall rain storm

squander waste

squelch crush, stifle

stagnant stale, motionless

staid demure, sedate

Quiz 32 (Analogies)

<u>Directions:</u> Choose the pair that expresses a relationship most similar to that expressed in the capitalized pair. Answers are on page 101.

1. Perspicacious : Insight ::

   (A) ardent : quickness
   (B) warm : temperature
   (C) wealthy : scarcity
   (D) rapacious : magnanimity
   (E) churlish : enmity

2. Unprecedented : Previous Occurrence ::

   (A) naive : harmony
   (B) incomparable : equal
   (C) improper : vacillation
   (D) eccentric : intensity
   (E) random : recidivism

3. SNAKE : INVERTEBRATE ::

   (A) dolphin : fish
   (B) eagle : talon
   (C) boa constrictor : backbone
   (D) penguin : bird
   (E) bat : insect

4. LIMERICK : POEM ::

   (A) monologue : chorus
   (B) sonnet : offering
   (C) waltz : tango
   (D) skull : skeleton
   (E) aria : song

5. INTEREST : OBSESSION ::

   (A) faith : caprice
   (B) nonchalance : insouciance
   (C) diligence : assiduity
   (D) decimation : annihilation
   (E) alacrity : procrastination

6. RESOLUTE : WILL ::

   (A) violent : peacefulness
   (B) fanatic : concern
   (C) balky : contrary
   (D) notorious : infamy
   (E) virtuous : wholesomeness

7. ATOM : MATTER ::

   (A) neutron : proton
   (B) vegetable : animal
   (C) molecule : element
   (D) component : system
   (E) pasture : herd

8. ACTORS : TROUPE ::

   (A) plotters : cabal
   (B) professors : tenure
   (C) workers : bourgeoisie
   (D) diplomats : government
   (E) directors : cast

9. COFFER : VALUABLES ::

   (A) mountain : avalanche
   (B) book : paper
   (C) vault : trifles
   (D) sanctuary : refuge
   (E) sea : waves

10. LION : CARNIVORE ::

    (A) man : vegetarian
    (B) ape : ponderer
    (C) lizard : mammal
    (D) buffalo : omnivore
    (E) shark : scavenger

stalwart pillar, strong, loyal

stamina vigor, endurance

stanch loyal

stanchion prop, foundation

stanza division of a poem

stark desolate

startle surprise

stately impressive, noble

static inactive, immobile

statue regulation

staunch loyal

stave ward off

steadfast loyal

stealth secrecy, covertness

steeped soaked, infused

stenography shorthand

stentorian loud or declamatory in tone

sterling high quality

stern strict

stevedore longshoreman

stifle suppress

stigma mark of disgrace

stiletto dagger

stilted formal, stiff

stimulate excite

stint limit, assignment

stipend payment

stipulate specify, arrange

stodgy stuffy, pompous

stoic indifferent to pain or pleasure

stoke prod, fuel

stole long scarf

stolid impassive

stout stocky

strait distress

stratagem trick, military tactic

stratify form into layers

stratum layer

striate to mark with stripes

stricture censure, restriction

strife conflict

striking impressive, attractive

stringent severe, strict

strive endeavor

studious diligent

stultify inhibit, enfeeble

stunted arrested development

stupefy deaden, dumfound

stupendous astounding

stupor lethargy

stylize formalize, artificial artistic style

stymie hinder, thwart

suave smooth, charming

sub rosa in secret

subcutaneous beneath the skin

subdue conquer

subjugate suppress

sublet subcontract

sublimate to redirect forbidden impulses (usually sexual) into socially accepted activities

sublime lofty, excellent

sublunary earthly

submit yield, acquiesce

subordinate lower in rank

subsequent succeeding, following

subservient servile, submissive

subside diminish

subsidiary subordinate

subsidize financial assistance

substantiate verify

substantive substantial

subterfuge cunning, ruse

subterranean underground

subvert undermine

succor help, comfort

succulent juicy, delicious

succumb yield, submit

suffice adequate

suffrage vote

suffuse pervade, permeate

suggestive thought-provoking, risqué

sullen sulky, sour

sully stain

sultry sweltering

summon call for, arraign

sumptuous opulent, luscious

sunder split

sundry various

superb excellent

supercilious arrogant

supererogatory wanton, superfluous

superfluous overabundant

superimpose cover, place on top of

superintend supervise

superlative superior

supernumerary subordinate

supersede supplant

supervene ensue, follow

supervise oversee

supine lying on the back

supplant replace

supplication prayer

suppress subdue

surfeit overabundance

surly rude, crass

surmise to guess

surmount overcome

surname family name

surpass exceed, excel

surreal dreamlike

surreptitious secretive

surrogate substitute

surveillance close watch

susceptible vulnerable

suspend stop temporarily

sustenance food

susurrant whispering

suture surgical stitch

svelte slender

swank fashionable

swarthy dark (as in complexion)

Quiz 33 (Matching)

Match each word in the first column with its definition in the second column. Answers are on page 101.

1.	STAVE	A.	distress
2.	STEVEDORE	B.	diligent
3.	STRAIT	C.	ward off
4.	STUDIOUS	D.	longshoreman
5.	SUBJUGATE	E.	various
6.	SUBTERFUGE	F.	overabundant
7.	SUNDRY	G.	suppress
8.	SUPERFLUOUS	H.	cunning
9.	SUPINE	I.	dreamlike
10.	SURREAL	J.	lying on the back

---

swatch strip of fabric

sweltering hot

swivel a pivot

sybarite pleasure-seeker

sycophant flatterer, flunky

syllabicate divide into syllables

syllabus schedule

sylph a slim, graceful girl

sylvan rustic

symbiotic cooperative, working in close association

symmetry harmony, congruence

symposium panel (discussion)

symptomatic indicative

synagogue temple

syndicate cartel

syndrome set of symptoms

synod council

synopsis brief summary

synthesis combination

systole heart contraction

T

tabernacle temple

table postpone

tableau scene, backdrop

taboo prohibition

tabulate arrange

tacit understood without being spoken

taciturn untalkative

tactful sensitive

tactics strategy

tactile tangible

taint pollute

talion punishment

tally count

talon claw

tandem two or more things together

tang strong taste

tangential peripheral

tangible touchable

tantalize tease

tantamount equivalent

taper candle

tariff tax on imported or exported goods

tarn small lake

tarnish taint

tarry linger

taurine bull-like

taut tight

tautological repetitious

tawdry gaudy

technology body of knowledge

tedious boring, tiring

teem swarm, abound

temerity boldness

temperate moderate

tempest storm

tempestuous agitated

tempo speed

temporal pertaining to time

tempt entice

tenable defensible, valid

tenacious persistent

tendentious biased

tenement decaying apartment building

tenet doctrine

tensile stretchable

tentative provisional

tenuous thin, insubstantial

tenure status given after a period of time

tepid lukewarm

terminal final

terminology nomenclature

ternary triple

terpsichorean related to dance

terrain the feature of land

terrapin turtle

terrestrial earthly

terse concise

testament covenant

testy petulant

tether tie down

theatrics histrionics

theologian one who studies religion

thesaurus book of synonyms

thesis proposition, topic

thespian actor

thews muscles

thorny difficult

thrall slave

threadbare tattered

thrive prosper

throes anguish

throng crowd

throttle choke

thwart to foil

Quiz 34 (Matching)

Match each word in the first column with its definition in the second column. Answers are on page 101.

1.	SWATCH	A.	to foil
2.	SYNOD	B.	anguish
3.	TACIT	C.	concise
4.	TALON	D.	provisional
5.	TAURINE	E.	agitated
6.	TEMPESTUOUS	F.	bull-like
7.	TENTATIVE	G.	claw
8.	TERSE	H.	understood without being spoken
9.	THROES	I.	council
10.	THWART	J.	strip of fabric

tiara crown

tidings news, information

tiff fight

timbre tonal quality, resonance

timorous fearful, timid

tincture trace, vestige, tint

tinsel tawdriness

tirade scolding speech

titan accomplished person

titanic huge

titer laugh nervously

tithe donate one-tenth

titian auburn

titillate arouse

titular in name only, figurehead

toady fawner, sycophant

tocsin alarm bell, signal

toil drudgery

tome large book

tonal pertaining to sound

topography science of map making

torment harass

torpid lethargic, inactive

torrid scorching, passionate

torsion twisting

torus doughnut shaped object

totter stagger

touchstone standard

tousled disheveled

tout praise, brag

toxicologist one who studies poisons

tractable docile, manageable

traduce slander

tranquilize calm, anesthetize

transcribe write a copy

transfigure transform, exalt

transfix impale

transfuse insert, infuse

transgression trespass, offense

transient fleeting, temporary

transitory fleeting

translucent clear, lucid

transpire happen

transpose interchange

trauma injury

travail work, drudgery

traverse cross

travesty caricature, farce

treatise book, dissertation

trek journey

trenchant incisive, penetrating

trepidation fear

triad group of three

tribunal court

tributary river

trite commonplace, insincere

troglodyte cave dweller

trollop harlot

troublous disturbed

trounce thrash

troupe group of actors

truckle yield

truculent fierce, savage

trudge march, slog

truism self-evident truth

truncate shorten

truncheon club

tryst meeting, rendezvous

tumbler drinking glass

tumefy swell

tumult commotion

turbid muddy, clouded

turgid swollen

turpitude depravity

tussle fight

tussock cluster of glass

tutelage guardianship

twain two

twinge pain

tyrannical dictatorial

tyranny oppression

tyro beginner

U

ubiquitous omnipresent, pervasive

ulterior hidden, covert

ultimatum demand

ululate howl, wail

umbrage resentment

unabashed shameless, brazen

unabated ceaseless

unaffected natural, sincere

unanimity agreement

unassuming modest

unavailing useless, futile

unawares suddenly, unexpectedly

unbecoming unfitting

unbridled unrestrained

Quiz 35 (Matching)

Match each word in the first column with its definition in the second column. Answers are on page 101.

1.	TIDINGS	A.	incisive
2.	TITER	B.	omnipresent
3.	TITULAR	C.	lethargic
4.	TORPID	D.	figurehead
5.	TRADUCE	E.	unrestrained
6.	TRENCHANT	F.	news
7.	UBIQUITOUS	G.	laugh nervously
8.	ULULATE	H.	ceaseless
9.	UNABATED	I.	wail
10.	UNBRIDLED	J.	slander

uncanny mysterious, inexplicable

unconscionable unscrupulous

uncouth uncultured, crude

unctuous insincere

undermine weaken

underpin support

underscore emphasize

understudy a stand-in

underworld criminal world

underwrite agree to finance, guarantee

undue unjust, excessive

undulate surge, fluctuate

unduly excessive

unequivocal unambiguous, categorical

unexceptionable beyond criticism

unfailing steadfast, unfaltering

unfathomable puzzling, incomprehensible

unflagging untiring, unrelenting

unflappable not easily upset

unfrock discharge

unfurl open up, spread out

ungainly awkward

uniformity sameness

unilateral action taken by only one party

unimpeachable exemplary

unison together

unkempt disheveled

unmitigated complete, harsh

unmoved firm, steadfast

unprecedented without previous occurrence

unremitting relentless

unsavory distasteful, offensive

unscathed unhurt

unseat displace

unseemly unbecoming, improper

unstinting generous

94

unsullied spotless, pure

unsung neglected, not receiving just recognition

untenable cannot be achieved

untoward perverse, unseemly

unwarranted unjustified

unwieldy awkward

unwitting unintentional

upshot result

urbane refined, worldly

ursine bear-like

usurp seize, to appropriate

usury lending money at high rates

utilitarian pragmatic, useful

utopia paradise

utter complete

uxorious a doting husband

V

vacillate waver

vacuous inane, empty

vagary whim

vain unsuccessful

vainglorious conceited

valediction farewell speech

valiant brave

validate affirm, authenticate

valor bravery

vanguard leading position

vanquish conquer

vapid vacuous, insipid

variance discrepancy

vassal subject, subordinate

vaunt brag

vehement adamant

venal mercenary, for the sake of money

vendetta grudge, feud

veneer false front, facade

venerable revered

venial excusable

venom poison, spite

venture risk, speculate

venturesome bold, risky

venue location

veracity truthfulness

veranda porch

verbatim word for word, literal

verbose wordy

verdant green, lush

verdict decision, judgment

vernacular common speech

vertigo dizziness

vestige trace, remnant

veto reject

vex annoy

viable capable of surviving, feasible

viaduct waterway

Quiz 36 (Matching)

Match each word in the first column with its definition in the second column. Answers are on page 101.

1.	UNCOUTH	A.	disheveled
2.	UNDULY	B.	capable of surviving
3.	UNFLAGGING	C.	awkward
4.	UNKEMPT	D.	uncultured
5.	UNSTINTING	E.	truthfulness
6.	UNTENABLE	F.	whim
7.	UNWIELDY	G.	unrelenting
8.	VAGARY	H.	cannot be achieved
9.	VERACITY	I.	generous
10.	VIABLE	J.	excessive

---

viand food

vicious evil, cruel

vicissitude changing fortunes

victuals food

vie compete

vigil watch, sentry duty

vigilant on guard

vignette scene

vigor vitality

vilify defame, malign

vindicate free from blame

vindictive revengeful

virile manly, strong

virtuoso highly skilled artist

virulent deadly, poisonous, infectious

visage facial expression

viscid thick, gummy

visitation a formal visit

vital necessary

vitiate spoil, ruin

vitreous glassy

vitriolic scathing

vituperative abusive, critical language

vivacious lively, high-spirited

vivid lifelike, clear

vivisection experimentation on animals, dissection

vocation occupation

vociferous adamant, clamoring

vogue fashion, chic

volant agile

volatile unstable, precarious

volition free will

voluble talkative

voluminous bulky, extensive

voracious hungry

votary fan, aficionado

vouchsafe confer, bestow

vulgarity obscenity

vulnerable susceptible

vulpine fox-like, cunning

W

wager bet
waggish playful
waive forego
wallow indulge
wan pale, pallid, listless
wane dissipate, wither
want need, poverty, lack of
wanton lewd, abandoned, gratuitous
warrant justification
wary guarded, cautious
wastrel spendthrift
waylay ambush, accost
wean remove from nursing, break a habit
weir dam
welter confusion, hodgepodge
wheedle to coax with flattery
whet stimulate
whiffle vacillate
whimsical capricious, playful
wield exercise control
willful deliberate, wanton
wily shrewd, crafty
wince cringe
windfall bonus, boon
winnow separate
winsome charmingly innocent
wistful sad yearning, melancholy
wither shrivel
wizened shriveled
woe anguish, despair

wont custom, habit
woo court, seek favor
wraith ghost
wrath anger, fury
wreak to inflict something violent
wrest snatch
wretched miserable
writ summons, court order
writhe contort, thrash about
wry twisted, ironic sense of humor

X

xenophillic attraction to strangers
xenophobia fear of foreigners
xylophone musical percussion instrument

Y

yarn story, tale
yearn desire strongly
yen desire, yearning
yore long ago
Young Turks reformers

Z

zeal earnestness, passion
zealot fanatic
zenith summit
zephyr gentle breeze

Quiz 37 (Sentence Completions)

Complete each sentence with the best available word. Answers are on page 101.

1. Though most explicitly sexist words have been replaced by gender-neutral terms, sexism thrives in the _____ of many words.

   (A) indistinctness
   (B) similitude
   (C) loquacity
   (D) implications
   (E) obscurity

2. The aspiring candidate's performance in the debate all but _____ any hope he may have had of winning the election.

   (A) nullifies
   (B) encourages
   (C) guarantees
   (D) accentuates
   (E) contains

3. She is the most _____ person I have ever met, seemingly with an endless reserve of energy.

   (A) jejune
   (B) vivacious
   (C) solicitous
   (D) impudent
   (E) indolent

4. Despite all its _____, a stint in the diplomatic core is invariably an uplifting experience.

   (A) merits
   (B) compensation
   (C) effectiveness
   (D) rigors
   (E) mediocrity

5. Robert Williams' style of writing has an air of _____: just when you think the story line is predictable, he suddenly takes a different direction. Although this is often the mark of a beginner, Williams pulls it off masterfully.

   (A) ineptness
   (B) indignation
   (C) reserve
   (D) jollity
   (E) capriciousness

6. Though a small man, J. Edgar Hoover appeared to be much larger behind his desk; for, having skillfully designed his office, he was _____ by the perspective.

   (A) augmented
   (B) comforted
   (C) apprehended
   (D) lessened
   (E) disconcerted

7. Existentialism can be used to rationalize evil: if one does not like the rules of society and has no conscience, he may use existentialism as a means of _____ a set of beliefs that are advantageous to him but injurious to others.

   (A) thwarting
   (B) proving
   (C) promoting
   (D) justifying
   (E) impugning

8. These categories amply point out the fundamental desire that people have to express themselves and the cleverness they display in that expression; who would have believed that the drab, mundane DMV would become the _____ such creativity?

   (A) catalyst for
   (B) inhibitor of
   (C) disabler of
   (D) referee of
   (E) censor of

9. This argues well that Erikson exercised less free will than Warner; for even though Erikson was aware that he was misdirected, he was still unable to _____ free will.

   (A) defer
   (B) facilitate
   (C) proscribe
   (D) prevent
   (E) exert

10. Man has no choice but to seek truth, he is made uncomfortable and frustrated without truth— thus, the quest for truth is part of what makes us _____ .

    (A) noble
    (B) different
    (C) human
    (D) intelligent
    (E) aggressive

Answers to Quizzes

Quiz 1	Quiz 2	Quiz 3	Quiz 4	Quiz 5	Quiz 6	Quiz 7	Quiz 8
1. I	1. E	1. B	1. A	1. J	1. E	1. A	1. E
2. G	2. B	2. F	2. C	2. I	2. A	2. J	2. B
3. E	3. D	3. G	3. E	3. H	3. C	3. I	3. D
4. F	4. A	4. H	4. A	4. G	4. E	4. E	4. E
5. C	5. E	5. E	5. A	5. F	5. D	5. D	5. E
6. D	6. A	6. A	6. E	6. E	6. A	6. G	6 E
7. B	7. C	7. C	7. A	7. D	7. C	7. F	7. C
8. J	8. D	8. D	8. B	8. C	8. B	8. H	8. E
9. A	9. B	9. J	9. C	9. B	9. E	9. C	9. D
10. H	10. A	10. I	10. C	10. A	10. B	10. B	10. C

Quiz 9	Quiz 10	Quiz 11	Quiz 12	Quiz 13	Quiz 14	Quiz 15	Quiz 16
1. B	1. B	1. D	1. A	1. B	1. D	1. J	1. B
2. A	2. C	2. J	2. B	2. A	2. E	2. I	2. E
3. D	3. D	3. I	3. D	3. J	3. B	3. H	3. A
4. C	4. A	4. A	4. D	4. H	4. B	4. G	4. E
5. F	5. E	5. F	5. A	5. I	5. C	5. F	5. D
6. E	6. B	6. E	6. B	6. G	6. D	6. E	6. A
7. H	7. C	7. H	7. C	7. F	7. C	7. D	7. E
8. G	8. A	8. G	8. A	8. D	8. C	8. C	8. B
9. J	9. B	9. C	9. D	9. E	9. B	9. B	9. D
10. I	10. E	10. B	10. B	10. C	10. C	10. A	10. C

Quiz 17	Quiz 18	Quiz 19	Quiz 20	Quiz 21	Quiz 22	Quiz 23	Quiz 24
1. E	1. D	1. D	1. A	1. J	1. E	1. F	1. A
2. F	2. B	2. E	2. D	2. F	2. E	2. G	2. E
3. G	3. E	3. F	3. D	3. I	3. C	3. H	3. E
4. H	4. C	4. A	4. C	4. H	4. B	4. I	4. A
5. A	5. A	5. B	5. B	5. G	5. E	5. J	5. A
6. B	6. B	6. C	6. A	6. B	6. E	6. A	6. D
7. C	7. E	7. G	7. C	7. E	7. A	7. B	7. D
8. D	8. A	8. J	8. B	8. D	8. C	8. C	8. D
9. I	9. A	9. I	9. C	9. C	9. D	9. D	9. B
10. J	10. E	10. H	10. E	10. A	10. C	10. E	10. E

Quiz 25	Quiz 26	Quiz 27	Quiz 28	Quiz 29	Quiz 30	Quiz 31	Quiz 32
1. H	1. C	1. B	1. A	1. J	1. E	1. I	1. E
2. I	2. B	2. A	2. D	2. I	2. B	2. C	2. B
3. J	3. E	3. E	3. E	3. H	3. E	3. B	3. D
4. D	4. A	4. J	4. E	4. G	4. B	4. J	4. E
5. E	5. D	5. C	5. B	5. F	5. C	5. G	5. D
6. G	6. E	6. I	6. C	6. E	6. D	6. H	6. B
7. F	7. B	7. H	7. A	7. D	7. C	7. E	7. D
8. A	8. E	8. G	8. C	8. C	8. E	8. F	8. A
9. B	9. C	9. F	9. C	9. B	9. D	9. A	9. D
10. C	10. A	10. D	10. D	10. A	10. A	10. D	10. E

Quiz 33	Quiz 34	Quiz 35	Quiz 36	Quiz 37
1. C	1. J	1. F	1. D	1. D
2. D	2. I	2. G	2. J	2. A
3. A	3. H	3. D	3. G	3. B
4. B	4. G	4. C	4. A	4. D
5. G	5. F	5. J	5. I	5. E
6. H	6. E	6. A	6. H	6. A
7. E	7. D	7. B	7. C	7. D
8. F	8. C	8. I	8. F	8. A
9. J	9. B	9. H	9. E	9. E
10. I	10. A	10. E	10. B	10. C

Word Analysis

Word analysis (etymology) is the process of separating a word into its parts and then using the meanings of those parts to deduce the meaning of the original word. Take, for example, the word INTERMINABLE. It is made up of three parts: a prefix IN (not), a root TERMIN (stop), and a suffix ABLE (can do). Therefore, by word analysis, INTERMINABLE means "not able to stop." This is not the literal meaning of INTERMINABLE (endless), but it is close enough. For another example, consider the word RETROSPECT. It is made up of the prefix RETRO (back) and the root SPECT (to look). Hence, RETROSPECT means "to look back (in time), to contemplate."

Word analysis is very effective in decoding the meaning of words. However, you must be careful in its application since words do not always have the same meaning as the sum of the meanings of their parts. In fact, on occasion words can have the opposite meaning of their parts. For example, by word analysis the word AWFUL should mean "full of awe," or awe-inspiring. But over the years it has come to mean just the opposite—terrible. In spite of the shortcomings, word analysis gives the correct meaning of a word (or at least a hint of it) far more often than not and therefore is a useful tool.

Examples:

INDEFATIGABLE

Analysis: IN (not); DE (thoroughly); FATIG (fatigue); ABLE (can do)
Meaning: cannot be fatigued, tireless

CIRCUMSPECT

Analysis: CIRCUM (around); SPECT (to look)
Meaning: to look around, that is, to be cautious

ANTIPATHY

Analysis: ANTI (against); PATH (to feel); Y (noun suffix)
Meaning: to feel strongly against something, to hate

OMNISCIENT

Analysis: OMNI (all); SCI (to know); ENT (noun suffix)
Meaning: all-knowing

Following are some of the most useful prefixes, roots, and suffixes.

Prefixes

1. **ab**	from	aberration
2. **ad**—also **ac, af, ag, al, an, ap, ar, as, at**	to	adequate
3. **ambi**	both	ambidextrous
4. **an**—also **a**	without	anarchy
5. **anti**	against	antipathetic
6. **ante**	before	antecedent
7. **be**	throughout	belie
8. **bi**	two	bilateral
9. **cata**	down	catacomb
10. **circum**	around	circumscribe
11. **com**—also **con, col, cor, cog, co**	together	confluence
12. **contra**	against	contravene
13. **de**	down (negative)	debase
14. **deca**	ten	decathlon
15. **decem**	ten	decimal
16. **di**	two	digraph
17. **dia**	through, between	dialectic
18. **dis**	apart (negative)	disparity
19. **du**	two	duplicate
20. **dys**	abnormal	dysphoria
21. **epi**	upon	epicenter
22. **equi**	equal	equitable
23. **ex**	out	extricate
24. **extra**	beyond	extraterrestrial
25. **fore**	in front of	foreword
26. **hemi**	half	hemisphere
27. **hyper**	excessive	hyperbole
28. **hypo**	too little	hypothermia
29. **in**—also **ig, il, im, ir**	not	inefficient
30. **in**—also **il, im, ir**	in, very	invite, inflammable
31. **inter**	between	interloper
32. **intro**—also **intra**	inside	introspective

104

33. **kilo**	one thousand	kilogram
34. **meta**	changing	metaphysics
35. **micro**	small	microcosm
36. **mili**—also **milli**	one thousand	millipede
37. **mis**	bad, hate	misanthrope
38. **mono**	one	monopoly
39. **multi**	many	multifarious
40. **neo**	new	neophyte
41. **nil**—also **nihil**	nothing	nihilism
42. **non**	not	nonentity
43. **ob**—also **oc, of, op**	against	obstinate
44. **pan**	all	panegyric
45. **para**	beside	paranormal
46. **per**	throughout	permeate
47. **peri**	around	periscope
48. **poly**	many	polyglot
49. **post**	after	posterity
50. **pre**	before	predecessor
51. **prim**	first	primitive
52. **pro**	forward	procession
53. **quad**	four	quadruple
54. **re**	again	reiterate
55. **retro**	backward	retrograde
56. **semi**	half	semiliterate
57. **sub**—also **suc, suf, sug, sup, sus**	under	succumb
58. **super**—also **supra**	above	superannuated
59. **syn**—also **sym, syl**	together	synthesis
60. **trans**	across	transgression
61. **un**	not	unkempt
62. **uni**	one	unique

Roots

Root	Meaning	Example
1. **ac**	bitter, sharp	acrid
2. **agog**	leader	demagogue
3. **agri**—also **agrari**	field	agriculture
4. **ali**	other	alienate
5. **alt**	high	altostratus
6. **alter**	other	alternative
7. **am**	love	amiable
8. **anim**	soul	animadversion
9. **anthrop**	man, people	anthropology
10. **arch**	ruler	monarch
11. **aud**	hear	auditory
12. **auto**	self	autocracy
13. **belli**	war	bellicose
14. **ben**	good	benevolence
15. **biblio**	book	bibliophile
16. **bio**	life	biosphere
17. **cap**	take	caprice
18. **capit**	head	capitulate
19. **carn**	flesh	incarnate
20. **ced**	go	accede
21. **celer**	swift	accelerate
22. **cent**	one hundred	centurion
23. **chron**	time	chronology
24. **cide**	cut, kill	fratricide
25. **cit**	to call	recite
26. **civ**	citizen	civility
27. **cord**	heart	cordial
28. **corp**	body	corporeal

29. **cosm**	universe	cosmopolitan
30. **crat**	power	plutocrat
31. **cred**	belief	incredulous
32. **cur**	to care	curable
33. **deb**	debt	debit
34. **dem**	people	demagogue
35. **dic**	to say	Dictaphone
36. **doc**	to teach	doctorate
37. **dynam**	power	dynamism
38. **ego**	I	egocentric
39. **err**	to wander	errant
40. **eu**	good	euphemism
41. **fac**—also **fic, fec, fect**	to make	affectation
42. **fall**	false	infallible
43. **fer**	to carry	fertile
44. **fid**	faith	confidence
45. **fin**	end	finish
46. **fort**	strong	fortitude
47. **gen**	race, group	genocide
48. **geo**	earth	geology
49. **germ**	vital part	germane
50. **gest**	carry	gesticulate
51. **gnosi**	know	prognosis
52. **grad**—also **gress**	step	transgress
53. **graph**	writing	calligraphy
54. **grav**	heavy	gravitate
55. **greg**	crowd	egregious
56. **habit**	to have, live	habituate
57. **hema**—also **hemo**	blood	hemorrhage
58. **hetero**	different	heterogeneous
59. **homo**	same	homogenized

60. **hum**	earth, man	humble
61. **jac**—also **jec**	throw	interjection
62. **jud**	judge	judicious
63. **junct**—also **join**	combine	disjunctive
64. **jus**—also **jur**	law, to swear	adjure
65. **leg**	law	legislator
66. **liber**	free	libertine
67. **lic**	permit	illicit
68. **loc**	place	locomotion
69. **log**	word	logic
70. **loqu**	speak	soliloquy
71. **macro**	large	macrobiotics
72. **magn**	large	magnanimous
73. **mal**	bad	malevolent
74. **manu**	by hand	manuscript
75. **matr**	mother	matriarch
76. **medi**	middle	medieval
77. **meter**	measure	perimeter
78. **mit**—also **miss**	send	missive
79. **morph**	form, structure	anthropomorphic
80. **mut**	change	immutable
81. **nat**—also **nasc**	born	nascent
82. **neg**	deny	renegade
83. **nomen**	name	nominal
84. **nov**	new	innovative
85. **omni**	all	omniscient
86. **oper**—also **opus**	work	operative
87. **pac**—also **plais**	please	complaisant
88. **pater**—also **patr**	father	expatriate
89. **path**	disease, feeling	pathos
90. **ped**—also **pod**	foot	pedestal

91. **pel**—also **puls**	push	impulsive
92. **pen**	hang	appendix
93. **phil**	love	philanthropic
94. **pict**	paint	depict
95. **poli**	city	metropolis
96. **port**	carry	deportment
97. **pos**—also **pon**	to place	posit
98. **pot**	power	potentate
99. **put**	think	computer
100. **rect**—also **reg**	straight	rectitude
101. **ridi**—also **risi**	laughter	derision
102. **rog**	beg	interrogate
103. **rupt**	break	interruption
104. **sanct**	holy	sanctimonious
105. **sangui**	blood	sanguinary
106. **sat**	enough	satiate
107. **sci**	know	conscience
108. **scrib**—also **script**	to write	circumscribe
109. **sequ**—also **secu**	follow	sequence
110. **simil**—also **simul**	resembling	simile
111. **solv**—also **solut**	loosen	absolve
112. **soph**	wisdom	unsophisticated
113. **spec**	look	circumspect
114. **spir**	breathe	aspire
115. **strict**—also **string**	bind	astringent
116. **stru**	build	construe
117. **tact**—also **tang, tig**	touch	intangible
118. **techni**	skill	technique
119. **tempor**	time	temporal
120. **ten**	hold	tenacious
121. **term**	end	interminable

122. **terr**	earth	extraterrestrial
123. **test**	to witness	testimony
124. **the**	god	theocracy
125. **therm**	heat	thermodynamics
126. **tom**	cut	epitome
127. **tort**—also **tors**	twist	distortion
128. **tract**	draw, pull	abstract
129. **trib**	bestow	attribute
130. **trud**—also **trus**	push	protrude
131. **tuit**—also **tut**	teach	intuitive
132. **ultima**	last	penultimate
133. **ultra**	beyond	ultraviolet
134. **urb**	city	urbane
135. **vac**	empty	vacuous
136. **val**	strength, valor	valediction
137. **ven**	come	adventure
138. **ver**	true	veracity
139. **verb**	word	verbose
140. **vest**	clothe	travesty
141. **vic**	change	vicissitude
142. **vit**—also **viv**	alive	vivacious
143. **voc**	voice	vociferous
144. **vol**	wish	volition

Suffixes determine the part of speech a word belongs to. They are not as useful for determining a word's meaning as are roots and prefixes. Nevertheless, there are a few that are helpful.

Suffixes

Suffix	Meaning	Example
1. **able**—also **ible**	capable of	legible
2. **acy**	state of	celibacy
3. **ant**	full of	luxuriant
4. **ate**	to make	consecrate
5. **er, or**	one who	censor
6. **fic**	making	traffic
7. **ism**	belief	monotheism
8. **ist**	one who	fascist
9. **ize**	to make	victimize
10. **oid**	like	steroid
11. **ology**	study of	biology
12. **ose**	full of	verbose
13. **ous**	full of	fatuous
14. **tude**	state of	rectitude
15. **ure**	state of, act	primogeniture

Exercise:

Analyze and define the following words. Answers begin on page 113.

Example: **RETROGRADE**
Analysis: retro (backward);   grade (step)
Meaning: to step backward, to regress

1.   **CIRCUMNAVIGATE**
Analysis:
Meaning:

2.   **MISANTHROPE**
Analysis:
Meaning:

3.   **ANARCHY**
Analysis:
Meaning:

4.   **AUTOBIOGRAPHY**
Analysis:
Meaning:

5.   **INCREDULOUS**
Analysis:
Meaning:

6.   **EGOCENTRIC**
Analysis:
Meaning:

7.   **INFALLIBLE**
Analysis:
Meaning:

8.   **AMORAL**
Analysis:
Meaning:

9.   **INFIDEL**
Analysis:
Meaning:

10.   **NONENTITY**
Analysis:
Meaning:

11.   **CORPULENT**
Analysis:
Meaning:

12.   **IRREPARABLE**

    Analysis:
    Meaning:

13.   **INTROSPECTIVE**

    Analysis:
    Meaning:

14.   **IMMORTALITY**

    Analysis:
    Meaning:

15.   **BENEFACTOR**

    Analysis:
    Meaning:

16.   **DEGRADATION**

    Analysis:
    Meaning:

17.   **DISPASSIONATE**

    Analysis:
    Meaning:

18.   **APATHETIC**

    Analysis:
    Meaning:

Solutions to Exercise

1.   **CIRCUMNAVIGATE**

    Analysis: CIRCUM (around);   NAV (to sail);   ATE (verb suffix)
    Meaning: To sail around the world.

2.   **MISANTHROPE**

    Analysis: MIS (bad, hate);   ANTHROP (man)
    Meaning: One who hates all mankind.

3.   **ANARCHY**

    Analysis: AN (without);   ARCH (ruler);   Y (noun suffix)
    Meaning: Without rule, chaos.

4.   **AUTOBIOGRAPHY**

    Analysis: AUTO (self); BIO (life); GRAPH (to write); Y (noun suffix)
    Meaning: One's written life story.

5. **INCREDULOUS**

Analysis: IN (not); CRED (belief); OUS (adjective suffix)
Meaning: Doubtful, unbelieving.

6. **EGOCENTRIC**

Analysis: EGO (self); CENTR (center); IC (adjective suffix)
Meaning: Self-centered.

7. **INFALLIBLE**

Analysis: IN (not); FALL (false); IBLE (adjective suffix)
Meaning: Certain, cannot fail.

8. **AMORAL**

Analysis: A (without); MORAL (ethical)
Meaning: Without morals.

Note: AMORAL does not mean immoral; rather it means neither right nor wrong. Consider the following example: Little Susie, who does not realize that it is wrong to hit other people, hits little Bobby. She has committed an AMORAL act. However, if her mother explains to Susie that it is wrong to hit other people and she understands it but still hits Bobby, then she has committed an *immoral* act.

9. **INFIDEL**

Analysis: IN (not); FID (belief)
Meaning: One who does not believe (of religion).

10. **NONENTITY**

Analysis: NON (not); ENTITY (thing)
Meaning: A person of no significance.

11. **CORPULENT**

Analysis: CORP (body); LENT (adjective suffix)
Meaning: Obese.

12.   **IRREPARABLE**

    Analysis: IR (not);   REPAR (to repair);   ABLE (can do)
       Meaning: Something that cannot be repaired; a wrong so
         egregious it cannot be righted.

13.   **INTROSPECTIVE**

Analysis: INTRO (within);   SPECT (to look);   IVE (adjective suffix)
      Meaning: To look inward, to analyze oneself.

14.   **IMMORTALITY**

Analysis: IM (not);   MORTAL (subject to death);   ITY (noun ending)
      Meaning: Cannot die, will live forever.

15.   **BENEFACTOR**

Analysis: BENE (good);   FACT (to do);   OR (noun suffix [one who])
      Meaning: One who does a good deed, a patron.

16.   **DEGRADATION**

Analysis: DE (down—negative);   GRADE (step);   TION (noun suffix)
Meaning: The act of lowering someone socially or humiliating them.

17.   **DISPASSIONATE**

    Analysis: DIS (away—negative);   PASS (to feel)
    Meaning: Devoid of personal feeling, impartial.

18.   **APATHETIC**

  Analysis: A (without);   PATH (to feel); IC (adjective ending)
Meaning: Without feeling; to be uninterested. (The apathetic voters.)

Idiom & Usage

The field of grammar is huge and complex—tomes have been written on the subject. This complexity should be no surprise since grammar deals with the process of communication.

Usage concerns how we choose our words and how we express our thoughts: in other words, are the connections between the words in a sentence logically sound, and are they expressed in a way that conforms to standard idiom? We will study six major categories:

- **Pronoun Errors**
- **Subject-Verb Agreement**
- **Misplaced Modifiers**
- **Faulty Parallelism**
- **Faulty Verb Tense**
- **Faulty Idiom**

PRONOUN ERRORS

A pronoun is a word that stands for a noun, known as the antecedent of the pronoun. The key point for the use of pronouns is this:

• Pronouns must agree with their antecedents in both number (singular or plural) and person (1st, 2nd, or 3rd).

Example:

Steve has yet to receive his degree.

Here, the pronoun *his* refers to the noun *Steve*.

Following is a list of the most common pronouns:

PRONOUNS

Singular	Plural	Both Singular and Plural
I, me	we, us	any
she, her	they	none
he, him	them	all
it	these	most
anyone	those	more
either	some	who
each	that	which
many a	both	what
nothing	ourselves	you
one	any	
another	many	
everything	few	
mine	several	
his, hers	others	
this		
that		

Reference

- A pronoun should be plural when it refers to two nouns joined by *and*.

  Example:

  > Jane and Katarina believe *they* passed the final exam.

  The plural pronoun *they* refers to the compound subject *Jane and Katarina*.

- A pronoun should be singular when it refers to two nouns joined by *or* or *nor*.

  Faulty Usage

  > Neither Jane *nor* Katarina believes *they* passed
  > the final.

  Correct

  > Neither Jane *nor* Katarina believes *she* passed the final.

- A pronoun should refer to one and only one noun or compound noun.

  This is probably the most common pronoun error. If a pronoun follows two nouns, it is often unclear which of the nouns the pronoun refers to.

  Faulty Usage

  > The breakup of the Soviet Union has left *nuclear*
  > *weapons* in the hands of unstable, nascent
  > *countries*. It is imperative to world security that
  > *they* be destroyed.

  Although one is unlikely to take the sentence to mean that the countries must be destroyed, that interpretation is possible from the structure of the sentence. It is easily corrected:

  > The breakup of the Soviet Union has left *nuclear*
  > *weapons* in the hands of unstable, nascent
  > *countries*. It is imperative to world security that
  > ***these weapons*** be destroyed.

119

Faulty Usage

> In Somalia, *they* have become jaded by the
> constant warfare.

This construction is faulty because *they* does not have an
antecedent. The sentence can be corrected by replacing *they* with
people:

> In Somalia, *people* have become jaded by the
> constant warfare.

Better:

> The people of Somalia have become jaded by the
> constant warfare.

• In addition to agreeing with its antecedent in number, a pronoun
must agree with its antecedent in person.

Faulty Usage

> *One* enters this world with no responsibilities.
> Then comes school, then work, then marriage
> and family. No wonder, *you* look longingly to
> retirement.

In this sentence, the subject has changed from *one* (third person) to
you (second person). To correct the sentence either replace *one*
with *you* or vice versa:

> *You* enter this world with no responsibilities.
> Then comes school, then work, then marriage
> and family. No wonder, *you* look longingly to
> retirement.

> *One* enters this world with no responsibilities.
> Then comes school, then work, then marriage
> and family. No wonder, *one* looks longingly to
> retirement.

Drill I

In each of the following sentences, part or all of the sentence is underlined. The answer-choices offer five ways of phrasing the underlined part. If you think the sentence as written is better than the alternatives, choose A, which merely repeats the underlined part; otherwise choose one of the alternatives. Answers begin on page 142.

1. Had the President's Administration not lost the vote on the budget reduction package, his first year in office would have been rated an A.

   (A) Had the President's Administration not lost the vote on the budget reduction package, his first year in office would have been rated an A.

   (B) If the Administration had not lost the vote on the budget reduction package, his first year in office would have been rated an A.

   (C) Had the President's Administration not lost the vote on the budget reduction package, it would have been rated an A.

   (D) Had the President's Administration not lost the vote on its budget reduction package, his first year in office would have been rated an A.

   (E) If the President had not lost the vote on the budget reduction package, the Administration's first year in office would have been rated an A.

2. The new law requires a manufacturer to immediately notify their customers whenever the government is contemplating a forced recall of any of the manufacturer's products.

   (A) to immediately notify their customers whenever the government is contemplating a forced recall of any of the manufacturer's products.

   (B) to immediately notify customers whenever the government is contemplating a forced recall of their products.

   (C) to immediately, and without delay, notify its customers whenever the government is contemplating a forced recall of any of the manufacture's products.

   (D) to immediately notify whenever the government is contemplating a forced recall of any of the manufacturer's products that the customers may have bought.

   (E) to immediately notify its customers whenever the government is contemplating a forced recall of any of the manufacturer's products.

3. World War II taught the United States the folly of punishing a vanquished aggressor; so <u>after the war, they enacted the Marshall Plan to rebuild Germany.</u>
   (A) after the war, they enacted the Marshall Plan to rebuild Germany.
   (B) after the war, the Marshall Plan was enacted to rebuild Germany.
   (C) after the war, the Marshall Plan was enacted by the United States to rebuild Germany.
   (D) after the war, the United States enacted the Marshall Plan to rebuild Germany.
   (E) after the war, the United States enacted the Marshall Plan in order to rebuild Germany.

4. In the 1950's, integration was an anathema <u>to most Americans; now, however, most Americans accept it as desirable.</u>
   (A) to most Americans; now, however, most Americans accept it as desirable.
   (B) to most Americans, now, however, most Americans accept it.
   (C) to most Americans; now, however, most Americans are desirable of it.
   (D) to most Americans; now, however, most Americans accepted it as desirable.
   (E) to most Americans. Now, however, most Americans will accept it as desirable.

5. Geologists in California have discovered a fault near the famous San Andreas Fault, <u>one that they believe to be a trigger for</u> major quakes on the San Andreas.
   (A) one that they believe to be a trigger for
   (B) one they believe to be a trigger for
   (C) one that they believe triggers
   (D) that they believe to be a trigger for
   (E) one they believe acts as a trigger for

6. A bite from the tsetse fly invariably paralyzes <u>its victims unless an antidote is administered</u> within two hours.
   (A) <u>its victims unless an antidote is administered</u>
   (B) <u>its victims unless an antidote can be administered</u>
   (C) <u>its victims unless an antidote was administered</u>
   (D) <u>its victims unless an antidote is administered to the victims</u>
   (E) <u>its victims unless they receive an antidote</u>

SUBJECT-VERB AGREEMENT

Within a sentence there are certain requirements for the relationship between the subject and the verb.

- The subject and verb must agree both in number and person.

    Example:

    > We have surpassed our sales goal of one million dollars.

    Here, the first person plural verb *have* agrees with its first person plural subject *we*.

Note, ironically, third person <u>singular</u> verbs often end in *s* or *es*:

> He *seems* to be fair.

- Intervening phrases and clauses have no effect on subject-verb agreement.

    Example:

    > Only one of the President's nominees was confirmed.

    Here, the singular verb *was* agrees with its singular subject *one*. The intervening prepositional phrase *of the President's nominees* has no effect on the number or person of the verb.

- When the subject and verb are reversed, they still must agree in both number and person.

    Example:

    > *Attached are copies* of the contract.

Here, the plural verb *are attached* agrees with its plural subject *copies*. The sentence could be rewritten as

> *Copies* of the contract *are attached*.

123

Drill II

Answers and solutions begin on page 146.

1. The rising cost of government bureaucracy have made it all but impossible to reign in the budget deficit.
    (A) The rising cost
    (B) Since the rising costs
    (C) Because of the rising costs
    (D) The rising costs
    (E) Rising cost

2. In a co-publication agreement, ownership of both the material and its means of distribution are equally shared by the parties.
    (A) its means of distribution are equally shared by the parties.
    (B) its means of distribution are shared equally by each of the parties.
    (C) its means of distribution is equally shared by the parties.
    (D) their means of distribution is equally shared by the parties.
    (E) the means of distribution are equally shared by the parties.

3. The rise in negative attitudes toward foreigners indicate that the country is becoming less tolerant, and therefore that the opportunities are ripe for extremist groups to exploit the illegal immigration problem.
    (A) indicate that the country is becoming less tolerant, and therefore that
    (B) indicates that the country is becoming less tolerant, and therefore
    (C) indicates that the country is becoming less tolerant, and therefore that
    (D) indicates that the country is being less tolerant, and therefore
    (E) indicates that the country is becoming less tolerant of and therefore that

4. The harvest of grapes in the local valleys decreased in 1990 for the third straight year but were still at a robust level.
    (A) The harvest of grapes in the local valleys decreased in 1990 for the third straight year but were
    (B) The harvest of grapes in the local valleys began to decrease in 1990 for the third straight year but were
    (C) In 1990, the harvest of grapes in the local valleys decreased for the third straight year but were
    (D) The harvest of grapes in the local valleys decreased for the third straight year in 1990 but was
    (E) The harvest of grapes in the local valleys began decreasing in 1990 for the third straight year but was

5. Each of the book's protagonists—Mark Streit, Mary Eby, and Dr. Thomas—has a powerful, dynamic personality.

    (A) Each of the book's protagonists—Mark Streit, Mary Eby, and Dr. Thomas—has
    (B) Each of the book's protagonists—Mark Streit, Mary Eby, and Dr. Thomas—have
    (C) All the book's protagonists—Mark Streit, Mary Eby, and Dr. Thomas—has
    (D) Mark Streit, Mary Eby, and Dr. Thomas—the book's protagonists—each has
    (E) Each of the book's protagonists—Mark Streit, Mary Eby, and Dr. Thomas—could have had

MISPLACED MODIFIERS

*   As a general rule, a modifier should be placed as close as possible to what it modifies.

Example:

>   Following are some useful tips for protecting
>   your person and property from the FBI.

As written, the sentence implies that the FBI is a threat to your person and property. To correct the sentence put the modifier *from the FBI* next to the word it modifies, *tips*:

>   Following are some useful tips from the FBI for
>   protecting your person and property.

125

- When a phrase begins a sentence, make sure that it modifies the subject of the sentence.

    Example:

    > Coming around the corner, a few moments
    > passed before I could recognize my old home.

    As worded, the sentence implies that the moments were coming around the corner. The sentence can be corrected as follows:

    > As I came around the corner, a few moments
    > passed before I could recognize my old home.

    or

    > Coming around the corner, I paused a few
    > moments before I could recognize my old home.

Drill III

Answers and solutions begin on page 149.

1. By focusing on poverty, <u>the other causes of crime—such as the breakup of the nuclear family, changing morals, the loss of community, etc.—have been overlooked by sociologists.</u>

    (A) the other causes of crime—such as the breakup of the nuclear family, changing morals, the loss of community, etc.—have been overlooked by sociologists.

    (B) the other causes of crime have been overlooked by sociologists—such as the breakup of the nuclear family, changing morals, the loss of community, etc.

    (C) there are other causes of crime that have been overlooked by sociologists—such as the breakup of the nuclear family, changing morals, the loss of community, etc.

    (D) crimes—such as the breakup of the nuclear family, changing morals, the loss of community, etc.—have been overlooked by sociologists.

    (E) sociologists have overlooked the other causes of crime—such as the breakup of the nuclear family, changing morals, the loss of community, etc.

2. Using the Hubble telescope, previously unknown galaxies are now being charted.

   (A) Using the Hubble telescope, previously unknown galaxies are now being charted.
   (B) Previously unknown galaxies are now being charted, using the Hubble telescope.
   (C) Using the Hubble telescope, previously unknown galaxies are now being charted by astronomers.
   (D) Using the Hubble telescope, astronomers are now charting previously unknown galaxies.
   (E) With the aid of the Hubble telescope, previously unknown galaxies are now being charted.

3. The bitter cold the Midwest is experiencing is potentially life threatening to stranded motorists unless well-insulated with protective clothing.

   (A) stranded motorists unless insulated
   (B) stranded motorists unless being insulated
   (C) stranded motorists unless they are insulated
   (D) stranded motorists unless there is insulation
   (E) the stranded motorist unless insulated

4. Traveling across and shooting the vast expanse of the Southwest, in 1945 Ansel Adams began his photographic career.

   (A) Traveling across and shooting the vast expanse of the Southwest, in 1945 Ansel Adams began his photographic career.
   (B) Traveling across and shooting the vast expanse of the Southwest, Ansel Adams began his photographic career in 1945.
   (C) Having traveled across and shooting the vast expanse of the Southwest, in 1945 Ansel Adams began his photographic career.
   (D) Ansel Adams, in 1945 began his photographic career, traveling across and shooting the vast expanse of the Southwest.
   (E) In 1945, Ansel Adams began his photographic career, traveling across and shooting the vast expanse of the Southwest.

FAULTY PARALLELISM

- For a sentence to be parallel, similar elements must be expressed in similar form.

- When two adjectives modify the same noun, they should have similar forms.

    Example: The topology course was both *rigorous* and *a challenge*.

    Since both *rigorous* and *a challenge* are modifying *course*, they should have the same form:

    > The topology course was both *rigorous* and *challenging*.

- When a series of clauses is listed, the verbs in each clause must have the same form.

    Example: During his trip to Europe, the President will *discuss* ways to stimulate trade, *offer* economic aid, and *trying* to forge a new coalition with moderate forces in Russia.

    In this example, the first two verbs, *discuss* and *offer*, are active. But the third verb in the series, *trying*, is passive. The form of the verb should be active:

    > During his trip to Europe, the President will *discuss* ways to stimulate trade, *offer* economic aid, and *try* to forge a new coalition with moderate forces in Russia.

- When the first half of a sentence has a certain structure, the second half should preserve that structure.

    Example: *To acknowledge* that one is an alcoholic is *taking* the first and hardest step to recovery.

    The first half of the above sentence has an infinitive structure, *to acknowledge*, so the second half must have a similar structure:

    > *To acknowledge* that one is an alcoholic is *to take* the first and hardest step to recovery.

Drill IV

Answers and solutions begin on page 152.

1. Common knowledge tells us that sensible exercise and <u>eating properly will result</u> in better health.
   - (A) eating properly will result
   - (B) proper diet resulted
   - (C) dieting will result
   - (D) proper diet results
   - (E) eating properly results

2. This century began with <u>war brewing in Europe, the industrial revolution well-established, and a nascent communication age.</u>
   - (A) war brewing in Europe, the industrial revolution well-established, and a nascent communication age.
   - (B) war brewing in Europe, the industrial revolution surging, and a nascent communication age.
   - (C) war in Europe, the industrial revolution well-established, and a nascent communication age.
   - (D) war brewing in Europe, the industrial revolution well-established, and the communication age beginning.
   - (E) war brewing in Europe, the industrial revolution well-established, and saw the birth of the communication age.

3. It is often better <u>to try repairing an old car than to junk it.</u>
   - (A) to try repairing an old car than to junk it.
   - (B) to repair an old car than to have it junked.
   - (C) to try repairing an old car than to junking it.
   - (D) to try and repair an old car than to junk it.
   - (E) to try to repair an old car than to junk it.

4. <u>Jurassic Park, written by Michael Crichton, and which was first printed in 1988,</u> is a novel about a theme park of the future in which dinosaurs roam free.
   - (A) Jurassic Park, written by Michael Crichton, and which was first printed in 1988,
   - (B) Jurassic Park, written by Michael Crichton and first printed in 1988,
   - (C) Jurassic Park, which was written by Michael Crichton, and which was first printed in 1988,
   - (D) Written by Michael Crichton and first printed in 1988, Jurassic Park
   - (E) Jurassic Park, which was written by Michael Crichton and first printed in 1988,

129

FAULTY VERB TENSE

A verb has four principal parts:

1. **Present Tense**
   a.   Used to express present tense.

   > *He studies hard.*

   b.   Used to express general truths.

   During a recession, people are cautious about taking on more debt.

   c.   Used with *will* or *shall* to express future time.

   > *He will take the SAT next year.*

2. **Past Tense**
   a.   Used to express past tense.

   > *He took the SAT last year.*

3. **Past Participle**
   a.   Used to form the *present perfect tense*, which indicates that an action was started in the past and its effects are continuing in the present. It is formed using *have* or *has* and the past participle of the verb.

   > *He has prepared thoroughly for the SAT.*

   b.   Used to form the *past perfect tense*, which indicates that an action was completed before another past action. It is formed using *had* and the past participle of the verb.

   He had prepared thoroughly before taking the SAT.

   c.   Used to form the *future perfect tense*, which indicates that an action will be completed before another future action. It is formed using *will have* or *shall have* and the past participle of the verb.

   He will have prepared thoroughly before taking the SAT.

4. Present Participle (*-ing* form of the verb)

a. Used to form the *present progressive tense*, which indicates that an action is ongoing. It is formed using *is*, *am*, or *are* and the present participle of the verb.

> *He is preparing thoroughly for the SAT.*

b. Used to form the *past progressive tense*, which indicates that an action was in progress in the past. It is formed using *was* or *were* and the present participle of the verb.

> *He was preparing for the SAT.*

c. Used to form the *future progressive tense*, which indicates that an action will be in progress in the future. It is formed using *will be* or *shall be* and the present participle of the verb.

> *He will be preparing thoroughly for the SAT.*

PASSIVE VOICE

The passive voice removes the subject from the sentence. It is formed with the verb *to be* and the past participle of the main verb.

Passive:

> *The bill was resubmitted by the Senator.*

Active:

> *The Senator has resubmitted the bill.*

Unless you want to de-emphasize the doer of an action, you should favor the active voice.

Drill V

Answers and solutions begin on page 155.

1. In the past few years and to this day, many teachers of math and science had chosen to return to the private sector.
    (A) had chosen to return to the private sector.
    (B) having chosen to return to the private sector.
    (C) chose to return to the private sector.
    (D) have chosen to return to the private sector.
    (E) have chosen returning to the private sector.

2. Most of the homes that were destroyed in last summer's brush fires were built with wood-shake roofs.
    (A) Most of the homes that were destroyed in last summer's brush fires were
    (B) Last summer, brush fires destroyed most of the homes that were
    (C) Most of the homes that were destroyed in last summer's brush fires had been
    (D) Most of the homes that the brush fires destroyed last summer's have been
    (E) Most of the homes destroyed in last summer's brush fires were being

3. Although World War II ended nearly a half century ago, Russia and Japan still have not signed a formal peace treaty; and both countries have been reticent to develop closer relations.
    (A) have not signed a formal peace treaty; and both countries have been
    (B) did not signed a formal peace treaty; and both countries have been
    (C) have not signed a formal peace treaty; and both countries being
    (D) have not signed a formal peace treaty; and both countries are
    (E) are not signing a formal peace treaty; and both countries have been

4. The Democrats have accused the Republicans of resorting to dirty tricks by planting a mole on the Democrat's planning committee and then used the information obtained to sabotage the Democrat's campaign.
    (A) used the information obtained to sabotage
    (B) used the information they had obtained to sabotage
    (C) of using the information they had obtained to sabotage
    (D) using the information obtained to sabotage
    (E) to have used the information obtained to sabotage

IDIOM & USAGE

Accept/Except:

Accept means "to agree to" or "to receive." *Except* means "to object to" or "to leave out."

We will *accept* (receive) your manuscript for review.

No parking is allowed, *except* (leave out) on holidays.

Account for:

When explaining something, the correct idiom is *account for*:

We had to *account for* all the missing money.

When receiving blame or credit, the correct idiom is *account to*:

You will have to *account to* the state for your crimes.

Adapted to/for/from:

Adapted to means "naturally suited for." *Adapted for* means "created to be suited for." *Adapted from* means "changed to be suited for."

The polar bear is *adapted to* the subzero temperatures.

For any "New Order" to be successful, it must be *adapted for* the continually changing world power structure.

Lucas' latest release is *adapted from* the 1950 B-movie "Attack of the Amazons."

Affect/Effect:

Effect is a noun meaning "a result."

Increased fighting will be the *effect* of the failed peace conference.

Affect is a verb meaning "to influence."

The rain *affected* their plans for a picnic.

133

All ready vs. Already:

All ready means "everything is ready."

Already means "earlier."

Alot vs. A lot:

Alot is nonstandard; *a lot* is the correct form.

Among/Between:

Between should be used when referring to two things, and *among* should be used when referring to more than two things.

The young lady must choose *between* two suitors.

The fault is spread evenly *among* the three defendants.

Being that vs. Since:

Being that is nonstandard and should be replaced by *since*.

(Faulty)   *Being that* darkness was fast approaching, we had to abandon the search.

(Better)   *Since* darkness was fast approaching, we had to abandon the search.

Beside/Besides:

Adding an *s* to *beside* completely changes its meaning: *Beside* means "next to." *Besides* means "in addition."

We sat *beside* (next to) the host.

Besides (in addition), money was not even an issue in the contract negotiations.

Center on vs. Center around:

Center around is colloquial. It should not be used in formal writing.

(Faulty)   The dispute *centers around* the effects of undocumented workers.

(Correct)   The dispute *centers on* the effects of undocumented workers.

Conform to (not *with*):

> Stewart's writing does not *conform to* standard literary conventions.

Consensus of opinion:

Consensus of opinion is redundant: *consensus* means "general agreement."

Correspond to/with:

Correspond to means "in agreement with":

> The penalty does not *correspond to* the severity of the crime.

Correspond with means "to exchange letters":

> He *corresponded with* many of the top European leaders of his time.

Different from/Different than:

The preferred form is *different from*. Only in rare cases is *different than* acceptable.

> The new Cadillacs are very *different from* the imported luxury cars.

Double negatives:

> *(Faulty)*   *Scarcely nothing* was learned during the seminar.
>
> *(Better)*   *Scarcely anything* was learned during the seminar.

Doubt that vs. Doubt whether:

Doubt whether is nonstandard.

> *(Faulty)*   I *doubt whether* his new business will succeed.
>
> *(Correct)*   I *doubt that* his new business will succeed.

Farther/Further:

Use *farther* when referring to distance, and use *further* when referring to degree.

> They went no *further* (degree) than necking.
>
> He threw the discs *farther* (distance) than the top seated competitor.

Fewer/Less:

Use *fewer* when referring to a number of items. Use *less* when referring to a continuous quantity.

>In the past, we had *fewer* options.

>The impact was *less* than what was expected.

Identical with (not *to*):

>This bid is *identical with* the one submitted by you.

In contrast to (not *of*):

>In *contrast to* the conservative attitudes of her time, Mae West was quite provocative.

Independent of (not *from*):

>The judiciary is *independent of* the other branches of government.

Not only ... but also:

In this construction, *but* cannot be replaced with *and*.

>*(Faulty)*   Peterson is *not only* the top salesman in the department *and also* the most proficient.

>*(Correct)*   Peterson is *not only* the top salesman in the department *but also* the most proficient.

On account of vs. Because:

Because is always better than the circumlocution *on account of*.

>*(Poor)*   *On account of* his poor behavior, he was expelled.

>*(Better)*   *Because* he behaved poorly, he was expelled.

One another/Each other:

Each other should be used when referring to two things, and *one another* should be used when referring to more than two things.

> The members of the basketball team (more than two) congratulated *one another* on their victory.

> The business partners (two) congratulated *each other* on their successful first year.

Plus vs. And:

Do not use *plus* as a conjunction meaning *and*.

> *(Faulty)*   His contributions to this community are considerable, *plus* his character is beyond reproach.

> *(Correct)*   His contributions to this community are considerable, *and* his character is beyond reproach.

Note: *Plus* can be used to mean *and* so long as it is not being used as a conjunction.

> *(Acceptable)*   His generous financial contribution *plus* his donated time has made this project a success.

In this sentence, *plus* is being used as a preposition. Note that the verb *has* is singular because an intervening prepositional phrase (*plus his donated time*) does not affect subject verb agreement.

Regard vs. Regards:

Unless you are giving best wishes to someone, you should use *regard*.

> *(Faulty)*   In *regards* to your letter, we would be interested in distributing your product.

> *(Correct)*   In *regard* to your letter, we would be interested in distributing your product.

Regardless vs. Irregardless:

Regardless means "not withstanding." Hence, the "ir" in *irregardless* is redundant. *Regardless* is the correct form.

Retroactive to (not *from*):

The correct idiom is *retroactive to*:

> The tax increase is *retroactive to* February.

Speak to/with:

To *speak to* someone is to tell them something:

> We *spoke to* Jennings about the alleged embezzlement.

To *speak with* someone is to discuss something with them:

> Steve *spoke with* his friend Dave for hours yesterday.

The reason is because:

This structure is redundant. Equally common and doubly redundant is the structure *the reason why is because*.

> *(Poor)*   The *reason why* I could not attend the party *is because* I had to work.

> *(Better)*   I could not attend the party *because* I had to work.

Whether vs. As to whether:

The circumlocution *as to whether* should be replaced by *whether*.

> *(Poor)*   The United Nations has not decided *as to whether* to authorize a trade embargo.

> *(Better)*   The United Nations has not decided *whether* to authorize a trade embargo.

Whether vs. If:

Whether introduces a choice; *if* introduces a condition. A common mistake is to use *if* to present a choice.

> *(Faulty)*   He inquired *if* we had decided to keep the gift.

> *(Correct)* He inquired *whether* we had decided to keep the gift.

Drill VI

Answers and solutions begin on page 158.

1. Regarding legalization of drugs, I am not concerned so much by its potential impact on middle class America <u>but instead</u> by its potential impact on the inner city.

   (A) but instead
   (B) so much as
   (C) rather
   (D) but rather
   (E) as

2. Unless you maintain at least a 2.0 GPA, <u>you will not graduate medical school.</u>

   (A) you will not graduate medical school.
   (B) you will not be graduated from medical school.
   (C) you will not be graduating medical school.
   (D) you will not graduate from medical school.
   (E) you will graduate medical school.

3. <u>The studio's retrospective art exhibit refers back to</u> a simpler time in American history.

   (A) The studio's retrospective art exhibit refers back to
   (B) The studio's retrospective art exhibit harkens back to
   (C) The studio's retrospective art exhibit refers to
   (D) The studio's retrospective art exhibit refers from
   (E) The studio's retrospective art exhibit looks back to

4. <u>Due to the chemical spill, the commute into the city will be delayed by as much as 2 hours.</u>

   (A) Due to the chemical spill, the commute into the city will be delayed by as much as 2 hours.
   (B) The reason that the commute into the city will be delayed by as much as 2 hours is because of the chemical spill.
   (C) Due to the chemical spill, the commute into the city had been delayed by as much as 2 hours.
   (D) Because of the chemical spill, the commute into the city will be delayed by as much as 2 hours.
   (E) The chemical spill will be delaying the commute into the city by as much as 2 hours.

Points to Remember

1. A pronoun should be plural when it refers to two nouns joined by *and*.

2. A pronoun should be singular when it refers to two nouns joined by *or* or *nor*.

3. A pronoun should refer to one and only one noun or compound noun.

4. A pronoun must agree with its antecedent in both number and person.

5. The subject and verb must agree both in number and person.

6. Intervening phrases and clauses have no effect on subject-verb agreement.

7. When the subject and verb are reversed, they still must agree in both number and person.

8. As a general rule, a modifier should be placed as close as possible to what it modifies.

9. When a phrase begins a sentence, make sure that it modifies the subject of the sentence.

10. For a sentence to be parallel, similar elements must be expressed in similar form.

11. When two adjectives modify the same noun, they should have similar forms.

12. When a series of clauses is listed, the verbs must be in the same form.

13. When the first half of a sentence has a certain structure, the second half should preserve that structure.

14. A verb has four principal parts:

   I. Present Tense

   a. Used to express present tense.

   b. Used to express general truths.

   c. Used with *will* or *shall* to express future time.

   II. Past Tense

   a. Used to express past tense.

   III. Past Participle

   a. Use

   d to form the *present perfect tense*, which indicates that an action was started in the past and its effects are continuing in the present. It is formed using *have* or *has* and the past participle of the verb.

   b. Used to form the *past perfect tense*, which indicates that an action was completed before another past action. It is formed using *had* and the past participle of the verb.

   c. Used to form the *future perfect tense*, which indicates that an action will be completed before another future action. It is formed using *will have* or *shall have* and the past participle of the verb.

   IV. Present Participle (-*ing* form of the verb)

   a. Used to form the *present progressive tense*, which indicates that an action is ongoing. It is formed using *is*, *am*, or *are* and the present participle of the verb.

   b. Used to form the *past progressive tense*, which indicates that an action was in progress in the past. It is formed using *was* or *were* and the present participle of the verb.

   c. Used to form the *future progressive tense*, which indicates that an action will be in progress in the future. It is formed using *will be* or *shall be* and the present participle of the verb.

15. Unless you want to de-emphasize the doer of an action, you should favor the active voice.

Solutions to Drill I

1. Had the President's Administration not lost the vote on the budget reduction package, his first year in office would have been rated an A.

   (A) Had the President's Administration not lost the vote on the budget reduction package, his first year in office would have been rated an A.

   (B) If the Administration had not lost the vote on the budget reduction package, his first year in office would have been rated an A.

   (C) Had the President's Administration not lost the vote on the budget reduction package, it would have been rated an A.

   (D) Had the President's Administration not lost the vote on its budget reduction package, his first year in office would have been rated an A.

   (E) If the President had not lost the vote on the budget reduction package, the Administration's first year in office would have been rated an A.

Choice (A) is incorrect because *his* appears to refer to *the President*, but the subject of the subordinate clause is *the President's Administration*, not *the President*.

   Choice (B) changes the structure of the sentence, but retains the same flawed reference.

   In choice (C), *it* can refer to either *the President's Administration* or *the budget reduction package*. Thus, the reference is ambiguous.

   Choice (D) adds another pronoun, *its*, but still retains the same flawed reference.

   Choice (E) corrects the flawed reference by removing all pronouns. The answer is (E).

2. The new law requires a manufacturer <u>to immediately notify their customers whenever the government is contemplating a forced recall of any of the manufacturer's products.</u>

(A) to immediately notify their customers whenever the government is contemplating a forced recall of any of the manufacturer's products.

(B) to immediately notify customers whenever the government is contemplating a forced recall of their products.

(C) to immediately, and without delay, notify its customers whenever the government is contemplating a forced recall of any of the manufacture's products.

(D) to immediately notify whenever the government is contemplating a forced recall of any of the manufacturer's products that the customers may have bought.

(E) to immediately notify its customers whenever the government is contemplating a forced recall of any of the manufacturer's products.

Choice (A) is incorrect because the plural pronoun *their* cannot have the singular noun *a manufacturer* as its antecedent.

Although choice (B) corrects the given false reference, it introduces another one. *Their* can now refer to either *customers* or *government*, neither of which would make sense in this context.

Choice (C) also corrects the false reference, but it introduces a redundancy: *immediately* means "without delay."

Choice (D) corrects the false reference, but its structure is very awkward. The direct object of a verb should be as close to the verb as possible. In this case, the verb *notify* is separated from its direct object *customers* by the clause "*that the government is contemplating a forced recall of any of the manufacturer's products that.*"

Choice (E) is correct because the singular pronoun *its* has the singular noun *a manufacturer* as its antecedent. The answer is (E).

3. World War II taught the United States the folly of punishing a vanquished aggressor; so <u>after the war, they enacted the Marshall Plan to rebuild Germany.</u>

(A) after the war, they enacted the Marshall Plan to rebuild Germany.

(B) after the war, the Marshall Plan was enacted to rebuild Germany.

(C) after the war, the Marshall Plan was enacted by the United States to rebuild Germany.

    (D)   after the war, the United States enacted the Marshall Plan to rebuild Germany.

    (E)   after the war, the United States enacted the Marshall Plan in order to rebuild Germany.

Choice (A) is incorrect. Since *United States* is denoting the collective country, it is singular and therefore cannot be correctly referred to by the plural pronoun *they*.

    Choice (B) is not technically incorrect, but it lacks precision since it does not state who enacted the Marshall Plan. Further, it uses a passive construction: "*was enacted.*"

    Choice (C) states who enacted the Marshall Plan, but it retains the passive construction "*was enacted.*"

    Choice (E) is second-best. The phrase "*in order*" is unnecessary.

    Choice (D) corrects the false reference by replacing *they* with *the United States*. Further, it uses the active verb *enacted* instead of the passive verb *was enacted*. The answer is (D).

4.   In the 1950's, integration was an anathema <u>to most Americans; now, however, most Americans accept it as desirable.</u>

    (A)   to most Americans; now, however, most Americans accept it as desirable.

    (B)   to most Americans, now, however, most Americans accept it.

    (C)   to most Americans; now, however, most Americans are desirable of it.

    (D)   to most Americans; now, however, most Americans accepted it as desirable.

    (E)   to most Americans. Now, however, most Americans will accept it as desirable.

The sentence is not incorrect as written. Hence, the answer is choice (A).

    Choice (B) creates a run-on sentence by replacing the semicolon with a comma. Without a connecting word—*and, or, but*, etc.—two independent clauses must be joined by a semicolon or written as two separate sentences. Also, deleting "*as desirable*" changes the meaning of the sentence.

    Choice (C) uses a very awkward construction: *are desirable of it.*

    Choice (D) contains an error in tense. The sentence progresses from the past to the present, so the verb in the second clause should be *accept*, not *accepted*.

    Choice (E) writes the two clauses as separate sentences, which is allowable, but it also changes the tense of the second clause to the future: *will accept.*

5. Geologists in California have discovered a fault near the famous San Andreas Fault, <u>one that they believe to be a trigger for</u> major quakes on the San Andreas.
    (A) one that they believe to be a trigger for
    (B) one they believe to be a trigger for
    (C) one that they believe triggers
    (D) that they believe to be a trigger for
    (E) one they believe acts as a trigger for

Choice (A) is incorrect since the relative pronoun *that* is redundant: the pronoun *one*, which refers to the newly discovered fault, is sufficient.

Although choice (C) reads more smoothly, it still contains the double pronouns.

Choice (D) is incorrect. Generally, relative pronouns such as *that* refer to whole ideas in previous clauses or sentences. Since the second sentence is about the fault and not its discovery, the pronoun *that* is appropriate.

Choice (E) is very tempting. It actually reads better than choice (A), but it contains a subtle flaw. *One* is the direct object of the verb *believes* and therefore cannot be the subject of the verb *acts*. Since *they* clearly is not the subject, the verb *acts* is without a subject.

Choice (B) has both the correct pronoun and the correct verb form. The answer is (B).

6. A bite from the tsetse fly invariably paralyzes <u>its victims unless an antidote is administered</u> within two hours.
    (A) <u>its victims unless an antidote is administered</u>
    (B) <u>its victims unless an antidote can be administered</u>
    (C) <u>its victims unless an antidote was administered</u>
    (D) <u>its victims unless an antidote is administered to the victims</u>
    (E) <u>its victims unless they receive an antidote</u>

Choice (A) is incorrect since it is unclear whether the victim or the fly should receive the antidote.

Choice (B) is incorrect since *is* is more direct than *can be*.

Choice (C) is incorrect. A statement of fact should be expressed in the present tense, not the past tense.

Choice (D) is wordy. A pronoun should be used for the phrase *the victims*.

Choice (E) is the answer since *they* correctly identifies who should receive the antidote.

Solutions to Drill II

1. The rising cost of government bureaucracy have made it all but
    impossible to reign in the budget deficit.
    (A) The rising cost
    (B) Since the rising costs
    (C) Because of the rising costs
    (D) The rising costs
    (E) Rising cost

Choice (A) is incorrect because the plural verb *have* does not agree
with its singular subject *the rising cost*.

   Both (B) and (C) are incorrect because they turn the sentence into
a fragment.

   Choice (E) is incorrect because *rising cost* is still singular.

   Choice (D) is the correct answer since now the plural verb *have*
agrees with its plural subject *the rising costs*.

2. In a co-publication agreement, ownership of both the material and
    its means of distribution are equally shared by the parties.
    (A) its means of distribution are equally shared by the parties.
    (B) its means of distribution are shared equally by each of the
         parties.
    (C) its means of distribution is equally shared by the parties.
    (D) their means of distribution is equally shared by the parties.
    (E) the means of distribution are equally shared by the parties.

Choice (A) is incorrect. Recall that intervening phrases have no effect
on subject-verb agreement. In this sentence, the subject *ownership* is
singular, but the verb *are* is plural. Dropping the intervening phrase
clearly shows that the sentence is ungrammatical:

   *In a co-publication, agreement ownership are equally
   shared by the parties.*

   Choice (B) is incorrect. Neither adding *each of* nor interchanging
shared and *equally* addresses the issue of subject-verb agreement.

   Choice (D) contains a faulty pronoun reference. The antecedent
of the plural pronoun *their* would be the singular noun *material*.

   Choice (E) is incorrect since it still contains the plural verb *are*.
The answer is choice (C).

3. The rise in negative attitudes toward foreigners <u>indicate that the
    country is becoming less tolerant, and therefore that</u> the
    opportunities are ripe for extremist groups to exploit the illegal
    immigration problem.
    (A) indicate that the country is becoming less tolerant, and
         therefore that
    (B) indicates that the country is becoming less tolerant, and
         therefore
    (C) indicates that the country is becoming less tolerant, and
         therefore that
    (D) indicates that the country is being less tolerant, and therefore
    (E) indicates that the country is becoming less tolerant of and
         therefore that

Choice (A) has two flaws. First, the subject of the sentence *the rise* is
singular, and therefore the verb *indicate* should not be plural. Second,
the comma indicates that the sentence is made up of two independent
clauses, but the relative pronoun *that* immediately following *therefore*
forms a subordinate clause.

Choice (C) corrects the number of the verb, but retains the
subordinating relative pronoun *that*.

Choice (D) corrects the number of the verb and eliminates the
subordinating relative pronoun *that*. However, the verb *being* is less
descriptive than the verb *becoming*: As negative attitudes toward
foreigners increase, the country becomes correspondingly less tolerant.
Being does not capture this notion of change.

Choice (E) corrects the verb's number, and by dropping the
comma, makes the subordination allowable. However, it introduces the
preposition *of* which does not have an object: less tolerant of what?

Choice (B) both corrects the verb's number and removes the
subordinating relative pronoun *that*. The answer is (B).

4. <u>The harvest of grapes in the local valleys decreased in 1990 for the
    third straight year but were</u> still at a robust level.
    (A) The harvest of grapes in the local valleys decreased in 1990
         for the third straight year but were
    (B) The harvest of grapes in the local valleys began to decrease
         in 1990 for the third straight year but were
    (C) In 1990, the harvest of grapes in the local valleys decreased
         for the third straight year but were
    (D) The harvest of grapes in the local valleys decreased for the
         third straight year in 1990 but was

147

    (E)   The harvest of grapes in the local valleys began decreasing in 1990 for the third straight year but was

Choice (A) is incorrect since the singular subject *the harvest* requires a singular verb, not the plural verb *were*.

    Choice (B) is illogical since it states that the harvest began to decrease in 1990 and then it states that it was the third straight year of decrease.

    In choice (C) the plural verb *were* still does not agree with its singular subject *the harvest*.

    Choice (E) contains the same flaw as choice (B).

    Choice (D) has the singular verb *was* agreeing with its singular subject *the harvest*. Further, it places the phrase *in 1990* more naturally. The answer is (D).

5.   Each of the book's protagonists—Mark Streit, Mary Eby, and Dr. Thomas—has a powerful, dynamic personality.
    (A)   Each of the book's protagonists—Mark Streit, Mary Eby, and Dr. Thomas—has
    (B)   Each of the book's protagonists—Mark Streit, Mary Eby, and Dr. Thomas—have
    (C)   All the book's protagonists—Mark Streit, Mary Eby, and Dr. Thomas—has
    (D)   Mark Streit, Mary Eby, and Dr. Thomas—the book's protagonists—each has
    (E)   Each of the book's protagonists—Mark Streit, Mary Eby, and Dr. Thomas—could have had

The sentence is grammatical as written. The answer is (A).

    When *each*, *every*, or *many a* precedes two or more subjects linked by *and*, they separate the subjects and the verb is singular. Hence, in choice (B) the plural verb *have* is incorrect.

    Choice (C) is incorrect since the singular verb *has* does not agree with the plural subject *all*.

    When *each* follows a plural subject it does not separate the subjects and the verb remains plural. Hence, in choice (D) the singular verb *has* is incorrect.

    Choice (E) also changes the meaning of the original sentence, which states that the protagonist <u>do</u> have powerful, dynamic personalities.

Solutions to Drill III

1. By focusing on poverty, <u>the other causes of crime—such as the breakup of the nuclear family, changing morals, the loss of community, etc.—have been overlooked by sociologists.</u>

   (A) the other causes of crime—such as the breakup of the nuclear family, changing morals, the loss of community, etc.—have been overlooked by sociologists.

   (B) the other causes of crime have been overlooked by sociologists—such as the breakup of the nuclear family, changing morals, the loss of community, etc.

   (C) there are other causes of crime that have been overlooked by sociologists—such as the breakup of the nuclear family, changing morals, the loss of community, etc.

   (D) crimes—such as the breakup of the nuclear family, changing morals, the loss of community, etc.—have been overlooked by sociologists.

   (E) sociologists have overlooked the other causes of crime—such as the breakup of the nuclear family, changing morals, the loss of community, etc.

Choice (A) is incorrect since it implies that *the other causes of crime* are doing the focusing.

Choice (B) has the same flaw.

Choice (C) is incorrect. The phrase *by focusing on poverty* must modify the subject of the sentence, but *there* cannot be the subject since the construction *there are* is used to introduce a subject.

Choice (D) implies that *crimes* are focusing on poverty.

Choice (E) puts the subject of the sentence *sociologists* immediately next to its modifying phrase *by focusing on poverty*. The answer is (E).

2. Using the Hubble telescope, previously unknown galaxies are now being charted.
    (A) Using the Hubble telescope, previously unknown galaxies are now being charted.
    (B) Previously unknown galaxies are now being charted, using the Hubble telescope.
    (C) Using the Hubble telescope, previously unknown galaxies are now being charted by astronomers.
    (D) Using the Hubble telescope, astronomers are now charting previously unknown galaxies.
    (E) With the aid of the Hubble telescope, previously unknown galaxies are now being charted.

Choice (A) is incorrect because the phrase *using the Hubble telescope* does not have a noun to modify.

Choice (B) is incorrect because the phrase *using the Hubble telescope* still does not have a noun to modify.

Choice (C) offers a noun, *astronomers*, but it is too far from the phrase *using the Hubble telescope*.

In choice (E), the phrase *with the aid of the Hubble telescope* does not have a noun to modify.

Choice (D) offers a noun, *astronomers*, and places it immediately after the modifying phrase *using the Hubble telescope*. The answer is (D).

3. The bitter cold the Midwest is experiencing is potentially life threatening to stranded motorists unless well-insulated with protective clothing.
    (A) stranded motorists unless insulated
    (B) stranded motorists unless being insulated
    (C) stranded motorists unless they are insulated
    (D) stranded motorists unless there is insulation
    (E) the stranded motorist unless insulated

Choice (A) is incorrect. As worded, the sentence implies that the cold should be well insulated.

Choice (B) is awkward; besides, it still implies that the cold should be well insulated.

Choice (D) does not indicate what should be insulated.

Choice (E), like choices (A) and (B), implies that the cold should be well insulated.

Choice (C) is the answer since it correctly implies that the stranded motorists should be well insulated with protective clothing.

4. <u>Traveling across and shooting the vast expanse of the Southwest, in 1945 Ansel Adams began his photographic career.</u>

   (A) Traveling across and shooting the vast expanse of the Southwest, in 1945 Ansel Adams began his photographic career.

   (B) In 1945, Ansel Adams began his photographic career, traveling across and shooting the vast expanse of the Southwest.

   (C) Having traveled across and shooting the vast expanse of the Southwest, in 1945 Ansel Adams began his photographic career.

   (D) Ansel Adams, in 1945 began his photographic career, traveling across and shooting the vast expanse of the Southwest.

   (E) Traveling across and shooting the vast expanse of the Southwest, Ansel Adams began his photographic career in 1945.

Choice (A) has two flaws. First, the introductory phrase is too long. Second, the subject Ansel Adams should immediately follow the introductory phrase since it was Ansel Adams—not the year 1945—who was traveling and shooting the Southwest.

Choice (B) is incorrect because the phrase *"traveling across... Southwest"* is too far from its subject Ansel Adams. As written, the sentence seems to imply that the photographic career was traveling across and shooting the Southwest.

Choice (C) is inconsistent in verb tense. Further, it implies that Adams began his photographic career after he traveled across the Southwest.

Choice (D) is awkward.

The best answer is choice (E).

Solutions to Drill IV

1. Common knowledge tells us that sensible exercise and <u>eating properly will result</u> in better health.
   (A) eating properly will result
   (B) proper diet resulted
   (C) dieting will result
   (D) proper diet results
   (E) eating properly results

Choice (A) is incorrect since *eating properly* (verb-adverb) is not parallel to *sensible exercise* (adjective-noun).
   Choice (B) offers two parallel nouns, *exercise* and *diet*. However, a general truth should be expressed in the present tense, not in the past tense.
   Choice (C) is not parallel since it pairs the noun *exercise* with the gerund (a verb acting as a noun) *dieting*.
   Choice (E) makes the same mistake as choice (A).
   Choice (D) offers two parallel nouns—*exercise* and *diet*—and two parallel verbs—*tells* and *results*. The answer is (D).

2. This century began with <u>war brewing in Europe, the industrial revolution well-established, and a nascent communication age.</u>
   (A) war brewing in Europe, the industrial revolution well-established, and a nascent communication age.
   (B) war brewing in Europe, the industrial revolution surging, and a nascent communication age.
   (C) war in Europe, the industrial revolution well-established, and a nascent communication age.
   (D) war brewing in Europe, the industrial revolution well-established, and the communication age beginning.
   (E) war brewing in Europe, the industrial revolution well-established, and saw the birth of the communication age.

Choice (A) is incorrect. Although the first two phrases, *war brewing in Europe* and *the industrial revolution well-established*, have different structures, the thoughts are parallel. However, the third phrase, *and a nascent communication age*, is not parallel to the first two.
   Choice (B) does not make the third phrase parallel to the first two.
   Choice (C) changes the meaning of the sentence: the new formulation states that war already existed in Europe while the original sentence states that war was only developing.

Choice (E) is not parallel since the first two phrases in the series are noun phrases, but *saw the birth of the communication age* is a verb phrase. When a word introduces a series, each element of the series must agree with the introductory word. You can test the correctness of a phrase in a series by dropping the other phrases and checking whether the remaining phrase agrees with the introductory word. In this series, each phrase must be the object of the preposition *with*:

> This century began *with* <u>war brewing in Europe</u>
> This century began *with* <u>the industrial revolution well-established</u>
> This century began *with* <u>saw the birth of the communication age</u>

In this form, it is clear the verb *saw* cannot be the object of the preposition *with*.

Choice (D) offers three phrases in parallel form. The answer is (D).

3.   It is often better <u>to try repairing an old car than to junk it.</u>
   (A)   to try repairing an old car than to junk it.
   (B)   to repair an old car than to have it junked.
   (C)   to try repairing an old car than to junking it.
   (D)   to try and repair an old car than to junk it.
   (E)   to try to repair an old car than to junk it.

Choice (A) is incorrect since the verb *repairing* is not parallel to the verb *junk*.

In choice (B), the construction *have it junked* is awkward. Further, it changes the original construction from active to passive.

Choice (C) offers a parallel construction (*repairing/junking*), but it is awkward.

Choice (D) also offers a parallel construction (*repair/junk*), but the construction *try and* is not idiomatic.

Choice (E) offers a parallel construction (*repair/junk*), and the correct idiom—*try to*. The answer is (E).

4. Jurassic Park, written by Michael Crichton, and which was first printed in 1988, is a novel about a theme park of the future in which dinosaurs roam free.

    (A) Jurassic Park, written by Michael Crichton, and which was first printed in 1988,

    (B) Jurassic Park, written by Michael Crichton and first printed in 1988,

    (C) Jurassic Park, which was written by Michael Crichton, and which was first printed in 1988,

    (D) Written by Michael Crichton and first printed in 1988, Jurassic Park

    (E) Jurassic Park, which was written by Michael Crichton and first printed in 1988,

Choice (A) is incorrect since the verb *written* is not parallel to the construction *which was ... printed*.

Choice (B) is the correct answer since the sentence is concise and the verb *written* is parallel to the verb *printed*.

Choice (C) does offer a parallel structure (*which was written/which was printed*); however, choice (B) is more concise.

Choice (D) rambles. The introduction *Written by ... 1988* is too long.

Choice (E) also offers a parallel structure (*which was written/[which was] printed*); however, choice (B) again is more concise. Note that *which was* need not be repeated for the sentence to be parallel.

Solutions to Drill V

1. In the past few years and to this day, many teachers of math and science <u>had chosen to return to the private sector.</u>
    (A) had chosen to return to the private sector.
    (B) having chosen to return to the private sector.
    (C) chose to return to the private sector.
    (D) have chosen to return to the private sector.
    (E) have chosen returning to the private sector.

Choice (A) is incorrect because it uses the past perfect *had chosen*, which describes an event that has been completed before another event. But the sentence implies that teachers have and are continuing to return to the private sector. Hence, the present perfect tense should be used.

Choice (B) is incorrect because it uses the present progressive tense *having chosen*, which describes an ongoing event. Although this is the case, it does not capture the fact that the event began in the past.

Choice (C) is incorrect because it uses the simple past *chose*, which describes a past event. But again, the sentence implies that the teachers are continuing to opt for the private sector.

Choice (D) is the correct answer because it uses the present perfect *have chosen* to describe an event that occurred in the past and is continuing into the present.

Choice (E) is incorrect because it leaves the thought in the sentence uncompleted.

2. <u>Most of the homes that were destroyed in last summer's brush fires were</u> built with wood-shake roofs.
    (A) Most of the homes that were destroyed in last summer's brush fires were
    (B) Last summer, brush fires destroyed most of the homes that were
    (C) Most of the homes that were destroyed in last summer's brush fires had been
    (D) Most of the homes that the brush fires destroyed last summer's have been
    (E) Most of the homes destroyed in last summer's brush fires were being

Choice (A) is incorrect because the simple past *were* does not express the fact that the homes had been built before the fire destroyed them.

Choice (B) merely rearranges the wording while retaining the simple past *were*.

Choice (C) is the correct answer because it uses the past perfect *had been* to indicate that the homes were completely built before they were destroyed by the fires.

Choice (D) is incorrect because it uses the present perfect *have been*, which implies that the homes were destroyed before being built.

Choice (E) is incorrect. Although dropping the phrase *that were* makes the sentence more concise, the past progressive *were being* implies that the homes were destroyed while being built.

3.   Although World War II ended nearly a half century ago, Russia and Japan still <u>have not signed a formal peace treaty; and both countries have been</u> reticent to develop closer relations.

   (A)   have not signed a formal peace treaty; and both countries have been

   (B)   did not signed a formal peace treaty; and both countries have been

   (C)   have not signed a formal peace treaty; and both countries being

   (D)   have not signed a formal peace treaty; and both countries are

   (E)   are not signing a formal peace treaty; and both countries have been

The sentence is grammatical as written. The present perfect verb *have … signed* correctly indicates that they have not signed a peace treaty and are not on the verge of signing one. Further, the present perfect verb *have been* correctly indicates that in the past both countries have been reluctant to develop closer relations and are still reluctant. The answer is (A).

In choice (B), the simple past *did* does not capture the fact that they did not sign a peace treaty immediately after the war and still have not signed one.

Choice (C) is very awkward, and the present progressive *being* does not capture the fact that the countries have been reluctant to thaw relations since after the war up through the present.

In choice (D), the present tense *are* leaves open the possibility that in the past the countries may have desired closer relations but now no longer do.

In choice (E), the present progressive tense *are … signing*, as in choice (D), leaves open the possibility that in the past the countries may have desired closer relations but now no longer do.

4. The Democrats have accused the Republicans of resorting to dirty tricks by planting a mole on the Democrat's planning committee and then <u>used the information obtained to sabotage</u> the Democrat's campaign.
    (A) used the information obtained to sabotage
    (B) used the information they had obtained to sabotage
    (C) of using the information they had obtained to sabotage
    (D) using the information obtained to sabotage
    (E) to have used the information obtained to sabotage

Choice (A) is incorrect because the simple past *obtained* does not express the fact that the information was gotten before another past action—the sabotage.

Choice (B) is incorrect because *used* is not parallel to *of resorting*.

Choice (C) is correct because the phrase *of using* is parallel to the phrase *of resorting*. Further, the past perfect *had obtained* correctly expresses that a past action—the spying—was completed before another past action—the sabotage.

Choice (D) is incorrect because *using* is not parallel to *of resorting* and the past perfect is not used.

Choice (E) is incorrect because *to have used* is not parallel to *of resorting* and the past perfect is not used.

Solutions to Drill VI

1. Regarding legalization of drugs, I am not concerned so much by its potential impact on middle class America <u>but instead</u> by its potential impact on the inner city.
    (A)   but instead
    (B)   so much as
    (C)   rather
    (D)   but rather
    (E)   as

The correct structure for this type of sentence is *not so much by* _____ *as by* _____. The answer is (E).

2. Unless you maintain at least a 2.0 GPA, <u>you will not graduate medical school.</u>
    (A)   you will not graduate medical school.
    (B)   you will not be graduated from medical school.
    (C)   you will not be graduating medical school.
    (D)   you will not graduate from medical school.
    (E)   you will graduate medical school.

Choice (A) is incorrect. In this context, *graduate* requires the word *from*: "you will not *graduate from* medical school."

The use of the passive voice in choices (B) and (C) weakens the sentence.

Choice (D) is the answer since it uses the correct idiom *graduate from*.

Choice (E) changes the meaning of the sentence and does not correct the faulty idiom.

3. The studio's retrospective art exhibit <u>refers back to</u> a simpler time in American history.
    (A) The studio's retrospective art exhibit refers back to
    (B) The studio's retrospective art exhibit harkens back to
    (C) The studio's retrospective art exhibit refers to
    (D) The studio's retrospective art exhibit refers from
    (E) The studio's retrospective art exhibit looks back to

Choice (A) is incorrect. *Retrospective* means looking back on the past. Hence, in the phrase *refers back*, the word *back* is redundant.

Choice (B) is incorrect because *harkens back* is also redundant.

Choice (C) is correct. Dropping the word *back* eliminates the redundancy.

Choice (D) is incorrect because the preposition *from* is non-idiomatic.

Choice (E) is incorrect because *looks back* is also redundant.

4. <u>Due to the chemical spill, the commute into the city will be delayed by as much as 2 hours.</u>
    (A) Due to the chemical spill, the commute into the city will be delayed by as much as 2 hours.
    (B) The reason that the commute into the city will be delayed by as much as 2 hours is because of the chemical spill.
    (C) Due to the chemical spill, the commute into the city had been delayed by as much as 2 hours.
    (D) Because of the chemical spill, the commute into the city will be delayed by as much as 2 hours.
    (E) The chemical spill will be delaying the commute into the city by as much as 2 hours.

Choice (A) is incorrect. Although many educated writers and speakers begin sentences with *due to*, it is almost always incorrect.

Choice (B) is incorrect: it is both redundant and awkward.

Choice (C) is incorrect. The past perfect *had been delayed* implies the delay no longer exists. Hence, the meaning of the sentence has been changed.

Choice (D) is correct. In general, *due to* should not be used as a substitute for *because of, owing to, by reason of*, etc.

Choice (E) is incorrect. The future progressive *will be delaying* is unnecessary and ponderous. Had choice (E) used the simple future *will delay*, it would have been better that choice (D) because then it would be more direct and active.